MULTINATIONAL COMPANIES AND ECONOMIC CONCENTRATION IN EUROPE

Multinational Companies and Economic Concentration in Europe

FRANK FISHWICK
Cranfield School of Management

Gower

Published by
Gower Publishing Company Limited,
Gower House, Croft Road, Aldershot, Hampshire GU11 3HR, England.

Fishwick, Francis
    Multinational companies and economic
    concentration in Europe.
    1. International business enterprises — Europe
    2. Industrial concentration — Europe
    I. Title
    338.8'8'094   HD2755.5

ISBN 0-566-00361-9

Printed and bound in Great Britain by
Biddles Ltd, Guildford and King's Lynn

Contents

v

Preface

About ten years ago two features of the European economy first attracted widespread attention — an apparently continuing increase in the predominance of 'big business' and a growing share of industry in the hands of 'multinational companies', companies with production in a number of countries. This book reports an attempt to analyse and quantify these trends, with the aid of data now available.

The first chapter explains the significance of industrial concentration and the role in this process of multinational companies. Issues of policy within the European Economic Community are outlined.

The second chapter summarises available data about the association between multinational operations and business concentration, including the results of a series of studies published by the Commission of the European Communities relating to the evolution of concentration in selected industries of member countries. Most of this factual information relates to manufacturing industry. As far as data availability permits, this chapter examines evidence from all Western European countries. Because comprehensive data are published only for the United Kingdom, France and Germany most of the statistical analysis is confined to these countries.

We examine in the third chapter, the effects of dominance of industrial sectors by multinational firms on competition in product markets, on foreign trade, employment, wage levels and efficiency. We discuss their implications for governments, other national institutions and supranational authorities.

At the end of the book, in the fourth chapter, there is a summary of conclusions and a tentative forecast of possible future trends.

Acknowledgements

This work originally began as a joint venture with my former colleague Michael Allen, and a first draft was completed late in 1979. Shortly after that, a large volume of new evidence was published for the United Kingdom, France and Germany and analysis of this new evidence has led me not only to rewrite most of the report but also to modify the conclusions substantially. I must take responsibility for the new version but, at the same time, wish to express thanks to Mike Allen for his help in the early stages.

Among those who have helped in this work, especially in the extensive data analysis are Dulce Soares-Marques, (who worked as a research assistant for four months), and Edward Fishwick. Their much appreciated assistance is indicated by the use of 'we' in most of the text describing the statistical results. Nina Kecman's help with computer programming was also very valuable.

I am indebted to Dr. Michel Ghertman who suggested necessary changes to earlier drafts, in order to bring in new material; also to staff of the Commission of the European Communities, the Deutsche Bundesbank, the Statistisches Bundesamt and the French STISI who have guided us to the best sources of relevant information.

1 The economic significance of concentration

Introduction

Business concentration has long attracted the interest and attention of economists and governments. There have always been two basic reasons for this concern. Firstly, the control over the supply of a product by one firm, or by a group of firms acting in collusion, may imply dominance over consumers or 'monopoly power'. Secondly, such control may also give the firm (or group) dominance over suppliers of materials and over labour markets — a large number of people may depend for their livelihoods on decisions taken by a small number of individuals within the dominant organisation.

In more recent years, increasing attention has been paid to the form of industrial structure known as *oligopoly*, where production is controlled by a few (but more than one) firms. This form of structure is generally associated with particular forms of competition for sales and, to a lesser degree, with particular kinds of behaviour in the purchase of productive resources (see the following sections on 'Concentration and competition in the market for the product' and 'Concentration in the purchasing of productive resources.')

Many of the industries where concentration is measured are defined by the physical content of the product or the method of manufacture rather than the end use. Such physical and technical criteria form the basis of standard national and international classifications. Concentration is also measured within specified geographical areas, usually countries. The studies of concentration designed and published by the

Commission of the European Communities all relate to national industries. Only if substitutes are not available from other industries, or from other countries, does a high degree of such concentration imply restriction of consumer choice. For example, about 50% of paper production in the UK is supplied by four firms but over 60% of the country's consumption is imported and many paper products compete with substitutes made from plastics or textile fabrics.

The implications of concentration for consumers on the one hand and for suppliers of materials and for employees with specialist skills on the other hand, may differ considerably. The employment prospects of employees in the British paper industry depend very much on the prosperity and policies of the major companies, even though these cannot be said to dominate their customers. For this reason, these two possible effects of concentration are analysed separately in the following two sections.

Finally, in the final section on 'Diversification and total size,' we consider the significance of diversification as an influence on the competitive strength of a company, and refer to the importance of 'aggregate concentration', as opposed to concentration in any one sector.

Concentration and competition in the market for the product

Definition of the market

The main objective of most studies of business concentration has been to identify 'power over the market' (or 'dominance' or 'monopoly'). Article 86 of the Treaty of Rome prohibits abuse by one or more undertakings of a 'dominant position' within the Common Market, in so far as it may affect trade between member states. Definition of a 'dominant position' and of the 'relevant market', which is subject to this domination have long been topics of discussion among economists, including more recently those employed by the Commission of the European Communities.[1*] The measurement of dominance is discussed in the next sub section; definition of the market must be the first stage.

The classification of products for definition of a market must partly be related to end use.[2] For example, many drinks may now be sold in glass, plastic or metal containers and for the purpose of assessing market concentration, the supply of 'beverage containers' may be more meaningful than the 'glass industry' or 'small metal products'. The principle adopted in this form of market definition is that the products should be close substitutes for each other and should not be substitutes for

* See page 14 for notes.

2

products outside.

A paper presented to the 1977 Bruges seminar on EEC competition policy by De Jong questioned the use of end product substitution as the criterion for definition of the 'relevant market'. He pointed out that firms within an industry defined by the conventional, physical criteria often had supply flexibility, which meant that they could easily enter new end product markets. His conclusion was similar to an earlier one by Adelman[3] who asserted that, provided one is aware of the conceptual issues, 'commonsense will enable us to define a market', and who deplored the 'fatuous over-elaboration' of the subject.

In practice, the problems of definition have not been resolved. For example, does the very large share of the French market for branded cat and dog foods enjoyed by Mars Ltd[4] constitute a 'dominant position' — or should one take into account the fact that many owners prefer to feed their cats and dogs on foods other than branded products? Dominance of the markets for frozen food, instant coffee or margarine raises the same question — are these 'relevant markets'? Outside the food industry, one can question whether the high degree of concentration in the UK press creates a 'dominant position', when there is competition from both state owned and commercial radio and television. Another problem in the definition of a market relates to its geographical limits. In the early 1950s the use of national boundaries was in many cases justified by restrictions on imports — quantitative restrictions or high tariffs. With the establishment of the European Common Market many of these barriers to trade between member countries have been removed, although protection from non-member countries may in some cases be higher than before. Non-tariff barriers and nationalistic preferences are also significant in some countries within the EEC.[5]

Another factor in the geographical delimitation of a market is transport cost. Containerisation and other transport improvements, together with a general increase in value to bulk ratio have tended to reduce the relative importance of transport cost, but with certain bulky products such as cement, international trade remains low because of transport expense. Indeed in such cases, national markets may be too large for analysis of concentration, and the European Commission's study of the French cement industry examined regional concentration.[6]

When foreign trade is significant and/or where substitutes are available from other industries, there may be little relationship between the concentration of production in an industry and the range of choice available to consumers. This needs to be considered in assessing the degree of market dominance, which might be implied by concentration in a particular industrial sector.

The traditional approach to measurement and definition of monopoly power (or market dominance)

The term 'dominant position' in the Treaty of Rome has not been offici-ally defined; this avoids a problem which has long troubled economists. Most traditional attempts to define monopoly power (or 'dominance') start with a theoretical zero in the conceptual model of *perfect com-petition*. In this model there is a very large number of independent and equal firms producing identical products (an *atomistic* structure). These identical products are recognised as such by informed consumers, who have equal access to every product and have no preferences between them. There is also complete freedom of entry to the market — new firms can enter with no competitive disadvantage compared with existing firms. There is no collusion between firms within the market nor do any agreements exist with potential entrants.

From this summary of the theoretical zero, it is clear that monopoly power has many dimensions. These include *seller concentration*, a term which is used to describe both a reduction in the number of competing firms and inequality of size. Another dimension is the degree of product differentiation, resulting from real differences between the products of individual firms and/or differences in the consumers' perception created by advertising, goodwill or ease of access. A third dimension is the exis-tence of barriers to the entry of new competitors: such barriers may include the limited size of the total market in relation to the most eco-nomic scale of production, ownership or control by existing firms of essential supplies or outlets, or established preferences for existing brands. The fourth dimension of power over a market is the degree of collusion or agreement to restrict competition both between existing firms and with potential competitors not yet active within the market.

Although seller concentration is only one element in the concept of monopoly power, it is closely linked with some of the other elements. Economies of large scale production create concentration and also barri-ers to the entry of new competitors; reduction in the number of firms increases their interdependence and therefore increases also the facility and the motivation for collusion. However, even if concentration itself could be comprehensively and unambiguously measured, (see the final section on 'Diversification and total size'), concentration would not be synonymous with market dominance. In order to measure dominance it is necessary to consider also the other three dimensions — product differentiation, barriers to entry and collusion — because these features can vary between industries with similar degrees of concentration.

Because of the impossibility of combining the four dimensions to provide a composite measure of monopoly power, some economists have attempted to quantify abuse of monopoly power by examining profits. Departures from perfect competition, i.e. power over a market,

4

should in theory be reflected in higher prices and reduced total output. Under the theoretical conditions of perfect competition profits would tend to zero, or towards a minimum required to make it economic to remain in business. Authors have defined monopoly profits by such measures as:

$$\frac{\text{Sales turnover} - \text{total costs (including a return to capital)}[7]}{\text{Sales turnover}}$$

or

$$\frac{\text{Value added} - \text{labour costs}[8]}{\text{Value added}}$$

but have found little correlation between such ratios and the factors likely to create market power — concentration, barriers to entry.

This low correlation is not surprising: not only are there substantial difficulties in obtaining strictly comparable data for different firms but also there are several reasons why dominance need not be reflected in company profits. Part of the gains from the exploitation of such power may be received by employees — studies of data for the US, France, Belgium and the UK all show that wages are higher in concentrated industries. Monopoly power may also be reflected in higher rates of discretionary expenditure and management 'slack'. Particularly where governments keep a watchful eye on possible exploitation of monopoly positions, maximisation of short term profits may be inconsistent with the long term strategies of major companies.

This short critique of the traditional approach to definition and measurement of monopoly power has indicated major difficulties. Several authors have suggested that measurement of dominance as a departure from atomistic or perfect competition is not only impossible but is also irrelevant to the study of market power in the last quarter of the twentieth century. Their view is that analysis of market structure must be focused on the predominant form of structure — *oligopoly*, or 'competition among the few'.

The analysis of oligopoly

In the late 1940s a few well known economists advocated a new approach to the analysis of market power based on competition between a small number of major groups — the 'wrestling match' as it was described by Perroux.[9] The argument that an atomistic industrial structure would not be ideal even if it were possible was strongly urged by Schumpeter,[10] who asserted that the existence of oligopoly and even short term monopoly not only led to economies of scale but also encouraged technical progress and economic expansion. This view has been developed considerably by Dr. Remo Linda who initiated and has supervised the series of studies of concentration for the Commission of the European Communities.

In a 1972 paper,[11] Linda rejected the concept of perfect competition as a theoretical ideal because of its inconsistency with the earning of profits to finance product improvement and innovation. He regarded as 'competition', actions taken by individual major firms in attempts to secure advantages over competitors. Product differentiation he therefore described as a competitive strategy; the erection of barriers to entry was also an aspect of competition among what he described as 'major groups of development' (large, usually multinational enterprises). The creation of such barriers might be a powerful stimulus to substitution, innovation and technical progress. Business strategies which were regarded in traditional economics as restrictive, were thus seen by Linda as part of the process of competition.

What aspects of concentration should then give rise to public concern? What 'abuses of dominant positions', in the words of the Treaty of Rome, should public authorities view with concern? A quotation from another author, A. Hunter[12] suggests the answer to this question:

> Economists are properly appreciative of economies of scale and the importance of adequate finance for technological research and economic innovation but they are equally aware of the dangers of foreclosure of entry into an industry and of arbitrary pricing, the empire-building propensities of businessmen and *the risk of simple stagnation where no competition is there to stimulate*.

The italicised words identify the danger as also perceived by Linda — the danger of stagnation or rigidity. Policies pursued by firms with the aim of gaining competitive advantage form part of the continuing competitive process. Attempts at product differentiation can lead to competitive quality improvements; actions to create barriers to entry can stimulate the search for substitutes and product development. The danger occurs when major groups, having secured large shares of markets, cease to compete, when there is stagnation behind the barriers to entry against new competitors. Such stagnation or rigidity will, in Linda's view normally be reflected in constancy of market shares. It is this rigidity, reflecting explicit agreement or tacit *détente* between the small number of dominant producers, which should attract public attention.

Oligopoly has a distinctive feature — the interdependence of the small number of companies. This interdependence means that all would gain, at least in the short run, if competition between them were less vigorous. However, because of opportunities for further economies of scale or because of a desire on the part of those directing major companies for growth, competition tends to continue and, according to numerous studies, to take particular forms. Competition in industries dominated by a small number of major companies, tends to consist of aggressive action by one of the firms followed by defensive parallel action by the others. At the same time individual companies tend to be reluctant to initiate any changes which would make their products comparatively less attractive to the customers (e.g. price increases, lower quality or reduced advertising), in case their competitors do not follow suit.

This phenomenon is most evident in the occurrence of price wars. If one firm reduces prices in an attempt to increase sales, and if it is one of a small number of companies selling a homogeneous product, the firm's competitors are likely to follow suit. Every firm is then likely to suffer reduced turnover and profits, (unless the demand for the total product is price sensitive). Once prices are reduced, they tend to remain so because, in the absence of an effective agreement between companies, any single one fears the competitive disadvantage which will be suffered if competitors do not follow suit. A remarkable example of a price war of this kind has occurred intermittently in the retail supply of motor gasolene in the UK, since 1976. This was precipitated by excess of supply over demand following price rises in 1974 − 75 and 1979.

Although excess supply has led to occasional price wars in certain oligopolistic markets, such markets are not normally associated with price competition. Unless the management of a firm believes that it possesses some significant cost advantage over its competitors, which will prevent them from matching a price reduction, aggressive price cutting is likely to be perceived as a dangerous strategy. Price increases may also be deterred by the fear that competitors may not follow suit. For these two reasons, price stability is a feature of some markets dominated by a few large firms. However, tacit acceptance of certain guidelines for price increases tend to emerge among the oligopolists, e.g. *price leadership*, where all competitors relate their prices to those of one leading firm.

Although price competition tends to be rare under conditions of oligopoly, other forms of competition may persist, even though there are dangers that the strategies of competing firms may offset each other and that all firms will be adversely affected. The tyre industry (a world wide oligopoly) provides an example: competition has partly been through product improvements affecting both reliability and durability. The average life of a steel based radial tyre for a passenger car is between two and three times that of the crossply tyre which predominated in most of Europe ten years ago. Price increases have failed to compensate for this greater product life and the tyre industry has been affected in recent years by surplus capacity and low profitability.

The forms of competition in oligopolistic markets are the concern of governments and international organisations responsible for ensuring 'fair trading' or 'consumer protection', (often described by the American term *anti-trust authorities*). Price competition is usually regarded by such authorities as beneficial to the consumers, although restrictive agreements related to prices have in certain instances been accepted because of a need for stability of supply or some other overriding public benefit, for example the need to ensure the financing of minimum safety standards. Competition through product improvement tends to be viewed more warily: although we believe that few *anti-trust authorities* would view the competitive product improvements in the tyre industry as other than beneficial, such authorities have occasionally criticised the rates at which minor innovations have been introduced in certain consumer goods industries, leading to cost increases and ultimately higher prices.[13] The role of advertising in oligopolistic markets has also been heavily criticised. Although such advertising supports the media through which it is diffused, many economists see it as a misallocation of resources, as 'wasteful'. This view was expressed emphatically by Linda in his 1972 paper.[11]

The analysis of competition in markets dominated by a few large enterprises requires much more empirical work. In particular, there is insufficient understanding of the way in which the nature of competition is likely to change over time. As an industry reaches maturity, is the degree of competition of all forms likely to diminish, as firms recall previous adverse experiences? Is collusion — via explicit or tacit agreement, or via financial and managerial connections — likely to increase? Observation of financial and marketing agreements between multinational companies in Europe, (e.g. in frozen foods and in domestic electrical appliances), suggests that there is a trend towards such collusion. On the other hand, the studies of concentration undertaken for the EEC Commission have revealed instances where such arrangements have been rescinded by companies wishing to exploit a new competitive advantage. Only broad generalisations can be embodied in any theory of *oligopoly*. The nature of competition within this, (increasingly predominant), market structure and its implications for public policy require investigations specific to the market concerned.

Public policy and the 'abuse of dominance'

Community law The concluding remark of the last sub-section is consistent with public policy in the EEC and in some of the countries which have statutory control over monopoly power (such as the UK and Denmark). Article 86 of the Treaty of Rome refers to the prohibition of 'abuse of a dominant position'. A ruling by the European Court of Justice in 1973 indicated that the Commission of the European Communities must show proof that such abuse has taken place before any action is taken.

The ruling concerned the Continental Can Company, a group formed from European subsidiaries of the American Can Company Incorporated, based in New York, the leading world producer of metal containers. In 1971 the EEC Commission made a decision that this company's takeover of a Dutch packaging company, Thomassen en Drijver-Verblifa, coming after an earlier takeover of a West German firm, Schalbach-Lubeca-Werke, established a monopoly position for metal cans and metal bottle tops in certain areas of the Common Market. Subsequently, in January 1972, the Commission published its decision invoking Article 86 against the Continental Can Company, on the grounds that it had abused a dominant position held within the Common Market.

The case against Continental Can was based on allegations that, having achieved a dominant position in the German market (with shares varying from 50 to 90 per cent according to the type of product), it misused this position by acquiring a potential competitor in the German market. The takeover also gave it a virtual monopoly in Benelux. The result was the elimination of a large part of the competition in a substantial area of the Common Market. Continental Can was required by the Commission to submit proposals ending the infringement and was informed that its licensing agreements with companies in Community countries (except Luxembourg) were being investigated by the Commission. Continental Can appealed against the Commission's action and this appeal was upheld in February 1973 by the European Court of Justice, on the grounds that the Commission had failed to prove specifically which sections of the market had been abused to the detriment of consumers. This case illustrates a major difference between Article 86 of the Treaty of Rome (relating to 'abuse of a dominant position') and Article 85 which prohibits agreements aimed at preventing or restricting competition, in so far as these affect trade between Member States. The parties to an agreement which restricts competition, are required to prove a case for its exemption from the provisions of Article 85. In contrast, Article 86 does not prohibit a dominant position, only the *abuse* of such a position and the Continental Can case made it clear that the onus of proof of such abuse lay with the Commission.

Although the Court of Justice upheld Continental Can's appeal, it expressly upheld the Commission's interpretation of Article 86, namely that a merger *could be* an abuse of a dominant position and could therefore be prohibited.[14] The decision stimulated the formulation by the Commission of proposals for more effective control of business mergers in the European Community and the issue of a draft Regulation, still under consideration. This provides for compulsory advance notification of mergers of companies with aggregate (world wide) turnover above a specified limit, (originally 1000 units of accounts), and for prior authorisation by the Commission. In determining whether a merger is compatible with the principles of the Common Market, the Commission would have to regard its effects on concentration and competition, consumer choice and technical progress. As with a dominant position under Article 86, there would be no *a priori* assumption that a merger would be against the public interest.

Walsh and Paxton[15] were among the legal commentators who took the view that the issues arising from the interpretation of Article 86, specifically in the Continental Can case, 'focused attention on the conflict between the greater degree of concentration needed in the Community to enable it to compete in advanced technology markets and the obvious dangers of creating dominant positions through mergers.'

Laws in member countries. We have described the legal situation emerging in the EEC, whereby restrictive agreements are condemned in principle but market dominance (or the establishment of such dominance through mergers) is prohibited only when the authorities consider and can prove that it is against the public interest. A flexible policy towards business concentration, balancing the advantages of economies of scale and economic efficiency on the one hand, and monopoly power on the other hand, is reflected also in the national policies relating to monopolies and mergers in member countries.

In France, Germany, Denmark, Ireland and the UK parties to agreements restricting competition are required to prove their advantages to the consumer or the wider economy — otherwise all such agreements are illegal. In contrast, the existence or establishment of a monopoly is not deemed to be against the public interest in any of these countries, though its abuse may be prohibited.

In France, mergers require prior government approval but some are positively encouraged and may be assisted by tax advantages. In the German Federal Republic, monopolies or dominating positions are not illegal but the government has powers to control abuse of such positions. It also considers mergers above a certain size and may prohibit these if they reduce world competition substantially.

The relevant laws in Ireland and Denmark resemble closely those of the UK. The UK Monopolies and Mergers Commission is required by government to investigate alleged monopolies and to comment on whether monopoly power exists and *whether* its existence and/or abuse operate against the public interest. A similar consideration of the cases for and against is required in the reporting by the Commission on mergers referred to it.

It has been pointed out by Pickering[16] that in the UK in the 1960s one government organisation (the Industrial Reconstruction Corporation) was trying to reorganise industry into larger units, while another government institution, (the Monopolies and Mergers Commission), was delaying and in some cases, preventing moves to increase concentration because of possible market implications. This ambivalence extends to a broader public attitude towards big business — admiration of the economies of scale and technical progress, fear of its possible power over the consumer. We have shown that it is reflected in policies throughout the EEC.

Concentration in the purchasing of productive resources

Concentration of purchasing has attracted much less attention from economists than concentration of sales, but much of the discussion about multinational companies has focused on this aspect. If control of an industry, (defined conventionally by physical and technical criteria), is concentrated in a small number of firms then it is likely that this small number of firms will dominate, as purchasers, the markets for certain materials, components and services and also for some kinds of labour. The technical terms used by economists for concentration of purchasing are *monopsony* (one purchaser) and *oligopsony* (a few purchasers).

Dominance of the purchase of intermediate industrial products

Examples of purchaser dominance affecting suppliers of components, materials or business services occur in many industries.

Studies by the present author for the Commission of the European Communities into the vehicle components and textile industries have revealed some examples of such dominance. In the motor industry, the large vehicle producers acquire certain components and business services from a number of much smaller firms.[17] In textiles, purchaser concentration is found among large clothing and tailoring groups with multiple outlets who, at least until the restructuring of the industry, bought from widely scattered and numerous suppliers of fabric.[18]

In discussions with the supplier firms in both these industries, complaints were encountered about the use of superior bargaining strength by the big customers. These extended to matters such as delays in payment, cancellation of orders, inadequate help with the financing of inventories and downward pressure on prices. Because these small firms relied on continuing sales to their big customers, they were occasionally forced to accept terms which were only marginally profitable. Although allegations of this kind were denied by the major purchasers, (who pointed to their own interest in the financial stability of suppliers), there is little doubt that the predominance of large purchasers was one of the factors which stimulated the restructuring of the UK textile industry in the 1960s. The formation of the major textile groups, partly through the action of the man-made fibres producers, was in part a response to the structural weakness of the industry in relation to its customers.

In Europe, national boundaries are expected to become less important as barriers to trade in goods and services. As this process continues, concentration in national industries becomes less directly associated with dominance over consumer markets, or with dominance over suppliers of intermediate products; consumers may, (in principle), turn to imports — producers of intermediate products to exports. Mobility of labour, both internationally and even between regions of the same country, has increased much less than that of goods, and the predominance of major employers in certain labour markets has increased rather than diminished in recent years.

Oligopsony in a labour market is in some ways analogous to oligopoly in the sale of a product. If an industry is dominated by a few large employers, then, at least in countries with strong and effective trade union organisation, concessions made by one firm are likely to be demanded by the others. This feature is observed particularly in situations where the employers concerned are located in the same localities.

Monopsony, that is dominance of a labour market by one firm, is a fairly common feature in all parts of Europe, because labour markets tend to be geographically confined. The 'company town' has been a feature of industrial societies since the Industrial Revolution. When a national industry exhibits a high degree of concentration, it is likely that within some region of the country one firm will dominate the market for at least certain kinds of labour. This is one reason why governments in many countries have intervened to give financial assistance to companies to enable them to avoid or defer the closure of large factories.

We have discussed the reasons why economists and those responsible for economic policy are interested in concentration. What is the best way to measure concentration in order to identify some of the problems which have been defined? The difficulties of definition of the activity within which concentration is measured were discussed in the section on 'Concentration and competition in the market for the product', (pages 2–11). Appendix I considers the statistical measurement of concentration within the defined activity. The literature on this subject is considerable[2,19]; in Appendix I we summarise the indices used in this research.

Diversification and total size

In this chapter we have discussed the significance of concentration in product markets and in the markets for intermediate products and for labour. Appendix I briefly examines the ways in which concentration can best be measured, in order to assess the absolute and comparative importance of the largest enterprises. This discussion has been based on concentration within one industry or activity, and one country. This approach ignores the advantages which may be obtained by companies whose activities extend over a number of industries, 'conglomerates', and/or over a number of countries, 'multinationals'. These advantages arise from diversification and from global size rather than size in any one country.

Industrial and/or international diversification may give a company distinct advantages over non-diversified competitors of the same size. Not only are risks spread, so that in any single national industry the company may be able to contemplate greater risks than non-diversified competitors, but it always has a wider range of options available for investment. Cross subsidisation of activities in particular industries or countries may be achieved by any of a number of policies. Its global size is another reason why a conglomerate and/or multinational company may have a stronger competitive position in relation to non-diversified firms, which would be indicated by its representation in any one national industry. There are economies of scale in administration, research, publicity and ability to obtain finance, which are related to the total activities of an enterprise rather than those in any one national industry. Diversification and global size (two separate elements) are the sources of many competitive advantages enjoyed by multinational companies, discussed in greater detail in Chapters 2 and 3. It is important here to emphasise again that many studies of concentration have failed to recognise the need to identify the companies with activities outside the national industry examined, and their resulting competitive advantages.

Another feature which is overlooked in many studies of concentration is the degree of aggregate concentration which may result from the existence of major conglomerate enterprises. This feature appears to be particularly significant in Italy, where large sectors of industry appear to be controlled by large holding companies, with investments in numerous and varied activities.

Data on aggregate concentration could only be found for the UK and France. For the UK, Table 1.1 shows the percentage of sales, employment and net output attributed to the 100 largest enterprises, (with a separate ranking for each variable), in 1977, with comparative data for 1958 and 1968 for the latter two variables.

The 1977 data are from the Census of Production for that year[20]; those for 1958 and 1968 are quoted by Prais[21] and derived from the corresponding Census for each of those years. It is interesting to note that aggregate concentration, which had increased significantly in the 1960s, changed very little after 1968. The marked slowing down in the 1970s in the trend towards greater aggregate concentration was accompanied by a slowing down in individual sectors, a point developed in a recent work by Hart and Clarke.[22]

Table 1.1

Importance of 100 largest private manufacturing firms in the UK

First 100 enterprises in order of variable shown	Combined share of variable for all firms		
	1958	1968(%)	1977(%)
Sales and work done	n.a.	n.a.	46.3
Net output	32	41	41.2
Employment	27	37	36.7

In France in 1975 the 100 largest industrial enterprises accounted for about 25.5 per cent of employment and 28.5 per cent of industry sales.[23] These firms included a few large public utilities. These French data support the widely held view that aggregate concentration in the UK is greater than elsewhere in Europe. Comment in another French source about trends in concentration,[24] points to statistical evidence that the rate of increase slowed down considerably during the 1970s.

Notes

1   See: Schröter, H., 'La position dominante', and De Jong, H., 'The Relevant Market', in *La règlementation du monopole en droit communautère*, Collège d'Europe, Bruges, 1977.

2   See: De Bandt, J., *Mesures de la dimension des unités de production*, Cahiers IREP no. 1, Institut de Recherches en Economie de la Production, Nanterre 1970, pp. 16—20.

3   See: Adelman, M.A., 'The Measurement of Industrial Concentration', in *Review of Economics and Statistics,* North Holland Publishing Co., Amsterdam, 1951.

4   See: Rastoin, J.L., Ghersi, G., and Castagnos, M., *Etude sur l'évolution de la concentration de l'industrie alimentaire en France*, Commission des Communautés Européennes, Brussels, 1975.

5   See: Michalet, C.A., 'Pourquoi des firms multinationales?', in *Les multinationales*, Cahiers Français no. 190, La Documentation Française, Paris, 1979.

6   See: Angelier, J.P., *Etude sur l'évolution de la concentration dans l'industrie du ciment en France*, Commission des CE, Brussels, 1979.

7   See: Qualls, D., 'Concentration, Barriers to Entry and Long-Run Economic Profit Margins', in *Journal of Industrial Economics,* B.H. Blackwell, Oxford, 1972.

8   See: Hart, P.E. and Morgan, E., 'Market Structure and Economic Performance in the United Kingdom' in *Journal of Industrial Economics*, B.H. Blackwell, Oxford, 1973, Number 3, pp. 117—93.

9   See: Perroux, F., 'Esquisse d'une théorie de l'économie dominante' in *Economie Appliquée*, Genève, 1948. Also quoted by R. Linda in *Economie Appliquée*, 1972, p. 367.

10   See: Schumpeter, J., *Capitalism, Socialism and Democracy*, Allen and Unwin, London, 1947. Also reproduced in abstracts in: Alex Hunter, *Monopoly and Competition*, Penguin, Harmondsworth, 1969, pp. 40—66.

11   See: Linda, R., 'Concurrence Oligopolistique et Planification Concurrentielle Internationale', in *Economie Appliquée*, Genève, 1972, Archives de l'Isea, pp. 342—4.

12   See: Hunter, A., *Competition and the Law*, Allen and Unwin, London, 1966, p. 69.

13   See: Monopolies Commission (UK), *Report on the Supply of Household Detergents*, HMSO, London, 1966.

14   See: *Official Journal of European Communities*, Luxembourg, 21st August 1973, (judgement of Court of Justice of 21 February 1973).

15   See: Walsh, A.E. and Paxton, J., *Competition Policy, European and International Trends and Practice, 1975*, Macmillan, London, 1975, p. 127.

16   See: Pickering, J.B., *Industrial Structure and Market Conduct*, Martin Robertson, Oxford, p. 150.

17   See: House of Commons Expenditure Committee, 14th Report, *The motor vehicle industry*, (HC617), HMSO, London, 1975, p. 17.

18   See: Fishwick, F. and Cornu, R.B., *A Study of the Evaluation of Concentration in the United Kingdom Textile Industry*, Commission of the European Communities, Brussels, 1975, p. 34.

19   See: Vanlommel, E., de Brabanders, B., and Liabaers, D., 'Industrial Concentration in Belgium: Empirical Comparison of Alternative Seller Concentration Measures', in *Journal of Industrial Economics*, Documentation Française, Paris, 1977.

Rosenbluth, G., 'Measures of Concentration', in Miller, J.B., *Business Concentration and Price Policy*, National Bureau of Economic Research, USA, 1955.

Hall, M. and Tideman, N., 'Measures of Concentration' in *American Statistical Journal*, 1967.

Nelson, R.L. *Concentration in the Manufacturing Industries of the United States*, Yale University Press, 1963.

20   See: Business Statistics Office (UK): *Census of Production 1977: Summary Tables*, PA 1002, HMSO, London, 1980.

21   See: Prais, S.J., *The Evolution of Giant Firms in Britain*, Cambridge University Press, 1976.

22   See: Hart, P.E. and Clarke, R., *Concentration in British Industry 1935–75*, National Institute of Economic and Social Research, London.

23   See: Brocard, R., *Les Entreprises Françaises: Concentration de grandes entreprises des secteurs et des branches*, Collections E 64, INSEE, Paris, 1979, p. 16.

24   See: STISI. 'La concentration des Entreprises Industrielles de 1972 à 1976', *Documentation Française*, Paris, 1979.

2 Multinational companies and the process of industrial concentration

Introduction

In this chapter we examine the part played by multinational companies in industrial concentration. Are the activities of multinational firms predominantly in highly concentrated sectors? Does the intervention of the multinationals increase concentration? To what extent has dominance by multinationals of the same industry in different countries, led to international oligopolies, transcending the power of national governments and nationally based trade unions?

In the second section on 'Possible associations between multinational operations and industrial concentration' in this chapter, we explain our interpretation of the term 'multinational', and outline some of the previous research into the relationship between multinational operation and economic concentration. In the third section on 'European evidence — analysis by sector', we summarise the available evidence on these two elements in individual industries within Europe, and in the final section on 'Statistical analysis of the relationship between foreign participation and concentration', we present the results of statistical analysis of this cross sectional information, comparing these with earlier research findings.

Possible associations between multinational operations and industrial concentration

Definition of 'multinational'

The adjective 'multinational' is easier to use than to define. A recent article by Dr. Bernadette Madeuf of a French research institute devoted to the study of multinational business[1*] identified two interpretations of the word. One of these implies that the equity capital and the management of the company are drawn from several countries and that its organisational structure, strategies and planning are conceived on a global scale. This interpretation was adopted in Vernon's seminal article in 1967,[2] the other interpretation is less restrictive — Madeuf quotes an earlier definition by Michalet,[3] which may be translated as 'a large national enterprise which possesses or controls several subsidiaries engaged in *production* in several countries', (our emphasis).

As Madeuf points out, the latter definition leaves some questions unanswered. How many is 'several'? (Vernon's sample of 187 multinationals all had at least six overseas subsidiaries.[4]) Should one adopt the alternative criterion that production outside the country of origin should represent a significant proportion of the company's total activities? If so, what proportion is significant?

In practice, these problems of definition tend to resolve themselves for the empirical researchers. In our opinion, a definition based on the multinationality of the capital, the managers, the strategy and the whole 'ethos' of a company is impractical. If it were to be objectively applied, it would require considerable research before a sample of multinational companies could be selected.

In this book, I have used what I consider to be the most practical definition, that based on the existence of significant *production* outside the country of origin. 'Significant' must be loosely interpreted — the *absolute* size of foreign production may be important, not only the ratio of that production to the total activity of the firm.

Because *production* is easier to define for a manufacturing organisation than for most other commercial activities, almost all published research concerned with 'multinationals' has related to manufacturing industries. This is in some senses regrettable because some of the most conspicuous developments in recent years have been in the international expansion of large financial organisations.[5] However, very few data exist for non-manufacturing activities and this, together with the problem of definition makes investigation of such activities very difficult. Most of the factual evidence which we shall present also relates to manufacturing industry.

---

* See page 51 for notes.

The problems of defining 'multinationals' also diminish in practice because most statistical analysis based on 'host countries', (i.e. the countries in which foreign firms have invested), relates to the role of these *foreign owned firms*, rather than home-based multinationals. In the statistical research reported later in this chapter, I have attempted to assess the roles of both foreign-owned enterprises and home-based multinationals, but, in general, much more information is available from official sources about foreign participation. The quantitative analysis in the final section on 'Statistical analysis of the relationship between foreign participation and concentration' is, therefore, concerned primarily with the association between industrial concentration and the involvement of foreign enterprises. (The significance of the distinction between home-based multinational and non-multinational companies is discussed in Chapter 3).

Motives for multinational operation in Europe

In examining the relationship between the activities of multinationals in Europe and economic concentration, it is necessary to consider some of the motives for production within individual European countries by companies with headquarters elsewhere.

Most investment by foreign companies in individual European countries appears to have been stimulated by market considerations rather than by cost differences, and attention will be directed to this kind of multinational diversification.[6]

From work of previous authors it is possible to identify three major influences on a decision by a company to establish overseas production facilities:

The motive to exploit more fully intangible fixed assets, such as accumulated technical knowledge and product development of success in marketing. This motive for companies to establish production in foreign countries has been emphasised in research undertaken by Caves[7] in the early 1970s. His analysis of Canadian and UK data showed that in both countries foreign participation in individual industries was positively correlated with the ratio to sales, (in each industry), expenditure on advertising, research and development. Caves went on to argue that high expenditures on marketing and research and development were generally confined to large firms in oligopolistic industries.

A similar view was expressed by J.W. Vaupel.[8] His analysis showed that the majority of US companies which had established subsidiaries in developed countries were manufacturers of technologically advanced products or of branded consumer goods. Oligopoly within the USA was a feature of all these industries.

The comparative economics of local production and exporting to a foreign market. There are three major considerations in such a comparison:

1 *Costs of transport in relation to those of production.* The findings from, (not extensive), previous research into this aspect suggest that transport costs are not in practice a major consideration, except in the case of perishable foodstuffs; products with a low 'value to bulk' ratio, such as cement; or products which are dangerous or difficult to transport such as explosive gases.[9] An important factor in this comparison may be the existence of economies of scale in production. If these are substantial, firms may be deterred from operation of a large number of plants and may prefer to supply foreign markets by exports.

2 *Competitive advantages of local production over exporting.* One competitive advantage is the avoidance of tariffs and other forms of trade protection. Even where tariffs have been reduced or even eliminated, non-tariff trade protection may continue, e.g. through the more rigorous application to imports than to domestically produced goods of certain legal specifications relating to a product.

The formal abandonment of trading restrictions in the EEC has been followed by some increase in non-tariff barriers, some of them resulting from national legislation, others from institutional, organisational or social pressures. Franko[10] describes the institutional factors which have led to the operation of individual plants in three or more EEC countries by EEC based steel manufacturers. Ghertman and Siegmund[11] showed that widely divergent regulations on health and labelling continued to act as non-tariff barriers for many food products. Under 25% of new cars sold in France and Germany in 1979 were imported — this may reflect national dominance of the automobile distribution networks. Nationalistic attitudes of local customers may affect some products — this was given by 30% of French multinational companies, (participating in a 1973 survey), as one reason for their decision to establish subsidiaries outside France.[9]

Apart from avoiding the legal and cultural barriers to imports, the subsidiary established within a foreign market is likely to compete more efficiently than would be possible as an importer. Delivery and servicing are likely to be more effective and the company is likely to be more informed about factors affecting business within the country. It is sometimes difficult, however, to identify whether this greater competitive efficiency results directly from the proximity of production to the points of sale or whether it reflects greater commitment to the market by the firm which has invested capital in production facilities.

3 *The spreading of risks and financial advantages.* This brings us to the question of comparative risk in supplying a market by exports or by local production. The French survey already quoted showed that 35% of companies establishing foreign production affiliates were partly motivated by a desire to spread risks geographically. Some of these risks may relate to continuity of production in the face of industrial disputes; others may relate to the consequences of changes in fiscal policy of governments; another group of risks concerns possible variations in access to national markets for exporters.

By 'going multinational' a company may obtain a number of advantages, arising mainly from its geographical diversification. The ability to switch production in the event of substantial changes in comparative costs in different countries; the possibility of reducing the incidence of tax by exploiting to the full tax incentives offered by different countries; possibly greater bargaining power in dealings with governments and organised labour — all these are factors which may influence the decision to establish foreign subsidiaries rather than exporting to foreign markets. (Most of these 'strategic' advantages are discussed further in Chapter 3.)

'Defensive' foreign investment. If one of a small number of companies exporting to a foreign market establishes a production subsidiary within the country and consequently gains a competitive advantage, the other companies in the oligopoly may feel the need to follow, in order to protect their own business. This movement by other firms to establish production units in the country concerned, is likely to continue to the point where the foreign market is so fully exploited that further investment would imply operating at sub-optimal production volumes.[12]

The hypothesis that 'defensive oligopolistic reaction' is a major motive for investment in foreign countries, has implications which have been tested empirically by T. Knickerbocker, a participant in the Harvard Multinational Enterprise Project.[13]

Firstly, one would expect firms in the same industry to follow each other within a short period into any one country. Knickerbocker defined *clusters* of peak direct investment, each consisting of subsidiaries established in a three year period in one country, by firms in one industry. He found that such clusters included nearly half of 1,900 subsidiaries established by 187 US companies over the 20 years 1948-67.*

Secondly, one would expect such peak clusters to predominate in industries with moderately high rather than low or very high degrees of concentration. When concentration is low, the action of one firm in

* These are the 187 companies referred to on page 18.

establishing a foreign subsidiary has little impact on its competitors. When concentration is very high, there are several possible deterrents to defensive foreign investment. One of these may be the potential loss of economies of scale, which characterise some of these highly concentrated sectors.

Thirdly, (as Knickerbocker explained), if there are only two or three large and close rivals in an industry, there is pressure towards some collusion to avoid direct confrontation in foreign countries and towards parallel moves to different markets.

Finally, when one company dominates an industry the question of oligopolistic reaction does not arise. Knickerbocker's findings confirmed the expected relationship between 'peaking' of direct foreign investment and concentration. The predominance of the three year single-country clusters was greatest in industries with a small number of firms of similar size (but greater than three), — few enough to make the companies interdependent, but too many for collusion to be practical.

The probable impact of foreign owned subsidiaries on industrial concentration within host countries *

The first impact. The effects of the initial establishment of subsidiaries of foreign companies in a national market on industrial concentration depend partly on the previous industrial structure. In the preceding sub section we described previous research which had found that multinational operation was most common in industries producing technically advanced goods, or branded consumer goods associated with heavy advertising. The effects of the entry of foreign firms depend on whether these are joining an existing oligopoly of national firms, (or replacing a single firm monopoly), or whether they are introducing new products, or new ways of producing or selling them, to a more fragmented industry.

In the first case, (where the national industry is already highly concentrated), the entry of foreign firms may reduce the level of concentration. Indeed, as Caves' points out[7] only large enterprises may be able to break down the barriers to entry which protect the existing national firms, through heavy advertising and the establishment of distribution links. It should be pointed out again that the barriers most likely to keep out foreign firms, (apart from government intervention), are those based on economies of scale in production which have already been achieved by national firms.

The entry of foreign companies into already highly concentrated industries, appears to have been much less common in the past than

---

* This section draws heavily on Dunning's work.[14]

22

entry to a fragmented structure. Both Vaupel[8] and Knickerbocker[13] pointed out that most of the industries in which multinational operation had been established were at the time newer, expanding activities. 'Expectations about future demand apparently figure more heavily in foreign investment decisions than do perceptions of existing demand', as Knickerbocker said. The first entry by foreign companies into expanding national industries has tended to occur historically before those industries have become highly concentrated.

One example is the motor industry in Europe, where US firms entered fragmented national industries which had considerable product variety, often falling to achieve economies of scale and to develop mass markets. In processed foods, international operation has generally been associated with the introduction of standard, branded products into markets previously supplied by a large number of producers supplying unbranded commodities. In technologically advanced industries, the large multi-national enterprise has generally entered markets where local producers were operating on an insufficiently large enough scale to finance the research and commercial development of new products. The production of electronics (e.g. computers and domestic electronic equipment), agricultural machinery and pharmaceuticals has become dominated by multinationals for this reason.

There are some industries which were concentrated from their establishment, and the entry of foreign subsidiaries has reduced this concentration, in some cases replacing national near monopolies. One such industry is the production of tyres, where there is an international oligopoly and the main companies are producing in most major national markets.

Another particular example where the entry of foreign firms may reduce national concentration is the UK brewing industry. Most lager beer produced in the UK is brewed by domestic brewers under licence from French, Danish, Belgian or German firms. One Danish brewer, Carlsberg, has acquired production facilities in the UK and has been advertising its product as 'brewed by Danes'. If other foreign producers were to follow suit, this would be an instance where multinational operations might lead to reduced concentration — about 56% of beer sales in the UK in 1972 were obtained by the five largest firms.

The acquisition by a foreign company of a domestic firm facing closure may prevent an increase in concentration. Examples include the takeover of the Rootes motor company in the UK by Chrysler in 1966 and American Tobacco's acquisition of Gallahers Ltd. in 1968, (preventing a monopoly on the part of Imperial Tobacco).

This discussion shows that it is hard to generalise about the initial effect of entry by foreign firms into a domestic industry on the structure of that industry. The cases where large foreign firms have entered previously fragmented industries and created a tendency towards *oligopoly* are not necessarily more numerous than those where foreign firms have brought new competition into a local highly concentrated activity.

Subsequent changes in industrial structure. Once a foreign firm has established a production subsidiary within a national industry, two processes are likely to take place; one of these will reduce concentration of production, the other will increase it. The process which will tend to reduce concentration is the entry of other foreign firms as an *oligopolistic reaction*, (described in the previous section). Concentration will be increased if firms based within the host country respond by merging in order to meet the more effective competition from foreign industry in greater strength.

The number of other foreign enterprises likely to enter a national industry after the first foreign owned production subsidiary has been established, will vary positively with the degree of advantage gained from production within the market, compared with exporting. As explained in the previous section, it will vary negatively with the ratio of the optimum scale of production to the size of the market which it is intended to serve.

In some cases, the degree of advantage obtained by internal production is very large. For example, French legislation prohibits almost completely the importation of pharmaceuticals. The effect has been to attract most foreign pharmaceutical firms into France, so that in 1976, nearly 40% of French sales were by foreign owned firms, but concentration was much lower than in other European countries.

Defensive mergers by domestic firms in response to the entry of foreign competitors are clearly illustrated by the European motor industries before the Second World War, a process which has continued. Similar mergers, some of them encouraged by governments, have occurred in data processing, electrical engineering, (including domestic appliances), chemicals, plastics and rubber industries. The motive to merge is greatest where greater size will enable the domestic firms to undertake research and development on the scale of their foreign competitors, and to commercially launch their improved products. One marketing advantage resulting from size is the ability to offer a complete range of products which are compatible with each other. This advantage is, (for example), particularly important in the sale of data processing equipment, of electro-acoustic apparatus and other electronic systems.

The effects on concentration of the entry of foreign firms into national industries will also depend on the method adopted for entry. The acquisition of existing companies, both the initial and subsequent foreign entrants will create, (other things being equal), a greater tendency towards concentration than the establishment of new production facilities.

In a major investigation into the establishment by foreign firms of subsidiaries in Belgium, Van den Bulcke[15] pointed out that the Belgian government, while for many years encouraging such foreign investment, has offered attractive financial incentives for new establishments and has adopted a more negative attitude towards take-overs of Belgian firms. Only 180 of 621 subsidiaries included in this survey, (in 1968), had been taken over by their foreign parent and 38% of the remaining firms gave the fiscal advantages as a reason for the establishment of a new plant in Belgium.

This same study showed that, in a small country like Belgium, the establishment of large foreign companies may lead to dominant market positions. Although foreign owned subsidiaries accounted for around 25% of value added by Belgian industry, many of their activities related to final products and they accounted for 33% of industrial sales. 37% of these firms expressed the view that they had no significant competitor in the Belgian market.

Multinational operation within the Common Market

The establishment of the European Common Market was expected by some observers to lead to greater international division of labour within Europe and therefore to the elimination of small national plants owned by multinational companies based either within Europe or outside. In his analysis based on evidence up to 1971, (relating therefore, to the six original members of the EEC), Franko[10] pointed out that this form of rationalisation had not occurred. In many industries, (e.g. processing, general industrial machinery, paints and glass), multinational operation within the Common Market had increased rather than diminished.

Several factors explain this. They include the non-tariff barriers to trade and apparent nationalistic preferences exhibited by some consumers, to which we have already referred. Franko points out that language and 'taste' differences between countries may make it advantageous to be close to national markets, and that such advantages may best be realised by national production. This may partly explain multinational operation in heavily branded products such as soaps, detergents, cosmetics, certain processed foods and soft drinks. Transport costs are another factor in the case of certain foods; e.g. they may explain multinational production of frozen foods. Other obstacles to rationalisation involve the closure of national units, and the resistance of organised labour and commitments to national governments.

One explanation of multinational operation which does not contradict the assumption of disappearing national economic barriers within the Common Market, is the takeover by major groups of smaller firms in other countries. The acquisition by Philips of Italian domestic appliance companies and the agreement and the abortive take-over by AEG-

Telefunken of the Italian firm Zanussi, (see Chapter 3), are illustrations of a process of *oligopolisation* which is taking place in the domestic electrical appliance industry in the EEC. This process follows from the establishment of freer international trade in these products and the breakdown of barriers to the movement of capital.

Although the same companies operate plants in several countries of the EEC there has been some tendency for international specialisation by plant. The best known example of this has occurred in the US owned motor companies, which have 'Europeanised' their EEC operations. A similar development has occurred in the French and German agricultural machinery industries and in the production of tyres. These developments are described further in the next section in 'European evidence — analysis by sector'.

Some hypotheses concerning the relationship between foreign participation and industrial concentration

Before presenting some information about the relationships between foreign participation and industrial concentration in Europe, it would be useful to present some hypotheses which appear to emerge from this analysis.

Comparisons of the levels of foreign participation and concentration. It is clear that the levels of foreign participation and concentration need not be closely correlated.

Some industries are highly concentrated because of economies of large scale production. If domestic firms have already attained the size necessary to achieve these economies of scale, then it may be uneconomical for foreign firms to establish their own local production, because this would mean operation at sub-optimal size, at least until a substantial share of total industry sales were reached. Particularly in long established and slow flowing activities, high levels of concentration are sometimes found alongside low degrees of foreign participation. The domestic firms themselves are also less likely to have multinational operations in such industries.

At any point in time when the comparison is made, the structure of an industry may reflect stages in the processes of oligopolistic reaction (entry by other foreign firms) and defensive merging by domestic companies. The timing of these processes may vary between industries and this will reduce the correlation between levels of foreign participation and concentration at any single time.

Finally, American researchers have shown that US companies usually enter industries serving expanding markets. Such markets tend to be dynamic rather than static and during the time of expansion are likely to be less concentrated than older, more mature sectors of the economy.

Therefore, although the foreign enterprises which establish subsidiaries in a given country are likely to be large companies, and to operate locally on a scale sufficient to permit exploitation of mass marketing at any point of time, the correlation between such foreign participation and industrial concentration may be weak.

Comparison of changes in concentration with the level of, (or changes in), foreign participation. Increases in concentration can occur for many reasons, in both declining and expanding industries. Among these are the exit of weaker firms at times of trading recession, and the mergers of firms to ensure survival under such trading conditions — neither of these are associated with industries recently entered by foreign enterprises. Mergers between subsidiaries of different foreign firms or between foreign subsidiaries and domestic companies, are also less likely than those between domestic companies for the purposes of jointly exploiting new production or marketing opportunities. These observations imply that subsidiaries of foreign firms tend to stand aside from some of the processes of concentration in domestic industry.

This last factor may offset some of the effects of foreign participation described earlier. It is not possible to build an *a priori* hypothesis about the likely degree of association between changes in industrial concentration and foreign participation.

European evidence — analysis by sector

Sources of data (See Appendix II for fuller details)

Until recently, discussion of the issues outlined in the last section has been hindered by lack of data.

For the *United Kingdom*, the country's Business Statistics Office produces annual data in considerable detail about business concentration both by industrial sector and by individual product; the amount of information published about foreign participation has decreased substantially since the 1968 Census.

For *France*, data both on concentration and on foreign involvement in individual industries have been published in considerable detail for the period since 1972. Some of these data appeared during the last few months of 1980. There is very little comparable material for before 1972.

Official institutions of the *German Federal Republic* have also begun to publish data of the kind needed to examine the hypotheses set out above only in very recent years. The Federal Statistical Office, (Statistisches Bundesamt), has included concentration ratios in its industrial Census analysis for the year 1977, for the first time. Comprehensive data on foreign investment in German industries were published for the first time in 1979 by the Federal Bank, (Bundesbank), — these related to 1976 and figures have also now been published for 1977.

Much of the previous statistical research into relationships between foreign participation and concentration was based exclusively on the UK. (This research is summarised in the final section of this chapter on 'Statistical analysis of the relationship between foreign participation and concentration'.) Lack of data makes it difficult to continue this research for years beyond 1968. Data for France and Germany are too recent to enable one to study the relationship between foreign investment and concentration over a period of years.

For other EEC countries there are insufficient data for detailed analysis of concentration and foreign participation by industrial sectors. An attempt to collect necessary data from information published by companies in annual accounts was frustrated by lack of detail for conglomerate multinational enterprises. This lack of 'transparency' is particularly, (and not unexpectedly), strong in oligopolistic industries.

One important source of evidence has been a series of studies of industrial concentration commenced in 1970 by the Directorate-General for Competition of the Commission of the European Communities. The principal purposes of these studies are the 'collection and analysis of information, viewed from the angle of competition'.[16] Reports have been published for a number of sectors and subsectors: most of these activities are discussed in the final section of this chapter. The undertaking of a study reflects an *a priori* view on the part of the Directorate-General for Competition, that the provisions of Article 86 of the Treaty of Rome might apply to the particular sector or subsector.

This series of studies has provided some useful data on concentration and on the role of multinational companies but these data remain incomplete, even for the selected industries. This is because some of the researchers in individual countries have been unable to obtain the required financial and other information. The investigators do not have authority to compel the provision of this information.

Summary information on foreign participation

A 1979 report by the Industry Committee of OECD[17] showed that most investment by foreign owned companies of member countries has been in manufacturing industries, although the proportion has fallen recently with investments associated with the exploitation of submarine oil deposits. Except in Italy, manufacturing accounted for well over half of foreign investment during the period 1960—74 in all the countries for which data are available.

Table 2.1 shows the total sales of subsidiaries of foreign owned firms, (defined as those in which the foreign holding exceeds 50%), as percenttages of sales by all manufacturing industries in the country concerned. The estimates relate to 1974 but are in some cases based on slightly earlier data.

Table 2.1

Sales by foreign owned subsidiaries as percentages of total sales by manufacturing industries, 1974

Over 20%		10 – 15%		Under 10%	
Belgium	44	UK	14	Denmark	8
Germany	25	Norway	13	Sweden	6
Austria	23	Spain	11	Finland	4
France	21				

Sources: OECD, *Penetration of Multinational Firms in the Manufacturing Industry of Member Countries*[17]
Belgian figure from Van den Bulcke, *The motives for disinvestment from EEC countries*[18]

The incomplete nature of Table 2.1 demonstrates the gaps in available information even about the total involvement of multinational firms in domestic industries.

Although the OECD report goes on to compare foreign penetration of individual industries in different countries, the gaps in the data and known inconsistencies of definition make it difficult to draw any conclusions. By combining the OECD material with evidence from the EEC Commission studies and the government statistics for France, Germany and the UK, it is possible to identify those sectors which are generally penetrated by multinational firms and those where such involvement is rare.

Table 2.2 is a summary based on these various sources of the shares of sales in major sectors of manufacturing industry achieved by subsidiaries, (and in some cases associated companies), of foreign companies.

The industrial pattern of foreign involvement is similar in all major European countries — to a greater degree than is indicated in Table 2.2. Within some of these broad industrial categories there are specific products which are generally associated with multinational companies.

Table 2.2

Latest data on foreign participation in manufacturing
sectors in France, Germany (FR), Italy and the UK
(% share of sales turnover)

	France	Germany	Italy	UK
Food & drink	16	18	21	13
Chemicals	30	26	23	30
Iron & steel	17	40 ⎫	9	11
Non-ferrous metals	10	28 ⎬		
Mechanical engineering	24	20 ⎭	25	20
Electrical goods	22	30	*	25
Motor vehicles & parts	17	24	5	36**
Textiles & clothing	9	7	21	6
Paper & products	17	14	19	17
Oil & natural gas	55	93	*	*

* = not available
** = estimated

Sources: (See Appendix Ii for further explanation)

France: Except for food, drink and tobacco the percentages are based on the *Indices de Pénétration Etrangère* published by the Statistics Division of the French Ministry of Industry.[19] The figures include the total turnover of majority owned firms; in addition, where the proportion of a domestic company's capital owned by a single foreign organisation lies between 20 and 50%, that share of the domestic company's turnover is included in the total. The data refer in principle to the year 1977. The percentages are also based on the EEC Commission study published in 1975 — data refer to 1973 and include only majority owned companies.[20]

Germany: Bundesbank statistics[21] for 1977. Data refer to turnover of all companies in which foreign participation, (single organisation), exceeds 25% of equity capital.

Italy: Data from OECD report supplemented by EEC Commission studies. Percentages refer in principle to 1974 and to majority owned subsidiaries.

UK: UK data are derived from Census of Production 1977, and refer to majority owned firms.

Analysis of concentration and multinational operations in individual sectors of manufacturing industry

Reports of the Commission of the European Communities[20] for France, Germany, Italy and the UK provide evidence both on foreign participation, and concentration in the food processing industry as a whole and in its constituent branches. Reports for other EEC countries contain fewer summary statistics.

Food processing. Table 2.3 shows the most recent available estimates of concentration and foreign involvement in food processing as a whole in each of the four countries.

Table 2.3

Concentration and Foreign Participation in the Food Industry

| | | Share of sales obtained by | |
		4 largest firms	Foreign owned firms
France	(1972)	8	16
Germany	(1977)	6	11
Italy	(1977)	25	21
UK	(1972)*	39	12

*Excludes drinks (included in other three countries). Note also that 'foreign owned firms' exclude Unilever (50% British), which accounted for about 10% of sales.
Sources: Reports published for EEC Commission[20]

The much higher level of concentration in the UK was due mainly to the domination by a small number of large firms of product markets, which in the three continental countries were much more fragmented. Such products include bread, flour and milk.

In all four countries, major international companies such as Unilever, Nestlé and Mars are strongly represented in certain common product markets. These include frozen foods, prepared infant foods, canned and packet soups, margarine and edible oils, chocolate and sugar confectionery, processed milk and soft cheeses, pet foods and instant coffee. Most of these have been expanding product markets dominated by heavily advertised brands.

The pattern of multinational involvement is not uniform. For example, Unilever is the leading company in frozen foods in the UK and Germany but does not sell frozen foods in France. One of its subsidiaries is a leading supplier of prepared soups in France but is not a major competitor in the UK. Nestlé and Unilever tend to avoid direct competition in

Germany,[22] and to some extent also in France, but compete in a number of products in the UK.

Comparison of concentration ratios over a time during the 1970s suggest that in food processing as a whole, concentration has tended to fall rather than increase, (see reference[22], p. 217). Data for individual products over a time are available only for the UK. In 22 of 36 product groups for which data have been published,[23] concentration increased between 1968 and 1975. There was no significant correlation among the 36 product groups, between the change in concentration and the degree of foreign participation.

Concentration in the supply of branded processed foods should be considered against the background of alternative foods. Many of the published statistics do not include very small firms which process foods for local distribution; many of the convenience products, in which seller concentration is high, can be replaced by domestic preparations. Food products have attracted very little attention on the part of anti-trust authorities, presumably for these reasons.

Alcoholic and non-alcoholic drinks. The Commission of the European Communities has published reports on concentration in the supply of drinks for most of the member countries.

These studies reveal that in most countries the supply of different drinks is becoming concentrated in the control of the same few firms. For example, in the UK the share of the four largest firms (Grand Metropolitan, Distillers, Allied Breweries, Bass Charrington) of total sales of beverages of all kinds rose from 52 to 59% between 1969 and 1974. French data for 1974, (no more recent information is available), show a four firm, (BSN, Pernod Ricard, Martini and Perrier), concentration ratio of 47%; in Denmark in 1975 the corresponding proportion had reached 85%. In contrast, concentration in Germany (FR), was very low — the four firm concentration ratio in 1973 was only 9%.

Similar contrasts were revealed for individual product markets. In the UK and France, concentration of supply was increasing up to 1975, but in Germany no such trend was apparent. For example, in 1975, three firms, (BSN, Heineken and Union de Brasserie), supplied 72% of beer produced in France,[24] while the five firm concentration ratio in the UK had reached 68%, having risen from 51% in 1963.[23] In Germany the three firm concentration ratio was only 10% in 1975.[22]

Since 1975 concentration in the supply of beer has fallen slightly in the UK, partly because of a recovery of brands other than those developed by high advertising expenditures and partly also because of the entry into the UK of a Danish competitor, Carlsberg.

Chemicals industries. Within this sector there are several groups of products for which demand has grown considerably over the past twenty years or so. These include basic chemicals (e.g. polymers and synthetic materials) and final products (pharmaceuticals, cosmetics, paints). The ratio of expenditure on research and development to sales, is generally above the average for manufacturing industry and many of the products are also associated with high expenditures on advertising and sales promotion.

Multinational operations are common in the chemicals industries, as indicated in Table 2.2. Concentration levels vary: nine of the '50 largest groups in Europe'[25] are primarily chemicals companies with interests in most branches of the industry. However, the perceived advantages of local operation, (sometimes stimulated by non-tariff barriers to trade), have led to fragmentation in some subsectors.

One example of such fragmentation is in *pharmaceuticals*. In France, in 1976 foreign owned firms accounted for about 39% of sales of pharmaceutical goods produced in France but there were no fewer than 87 such foreign firms, and the overall four firm, sales concentration ratio was only 11%.[19,26] A similar situation is revealed by data for West Germany, recently reported by the European Commission.[20] This shows for 1977, foreign participation of around 35% and a four firm, concentration ratio of about 22%. Data for the Italian pharmaceuticals industry, also for 1977, indicate foreign participation of about 51% and a four firm concentration of 26%.[20] In Belgium, research for the Commission revealed an industry dominated by foreign owned firms but with relatively low concentration.

It is important to emphasise that among pharmaceuticals and other products of the chemicals industry, there are specific product markets which may be highly concentrated or because of patents or economies of scale in production may be virtually captive to one firm. The case of the UK government versus Hoffman La Roche, which has received world-wide attention, illustrates this point very clearly.[26]

Table 2.4 contains summary estimates based on available data about concentration and foreign participation in the chemicals industry in the UK, France and Germany (FR).

Metals industries. In the iron and steel industry, multinational operation within the EEC results mainly from the operations in neighbouring countries by companies based in Belgium, Luxembourg and (to a lesser extent) West Germany. These activities in nearby foreign countries are attributed by Franko[10] to a desire to safeguard their business against the protectionist pressures which continue to affect steel production.

The shares of foreign owned companies and the concentration ratios in iron and steel production in France and Germany in the mid 1970s were as shown in Table 2.5.

Production of steel in West Germany is approximately equal to that of the UK and France combined and was about one third of that of the

Table 2.4

Sales concentration and foreign participation in chemicals

Country	Year	Subsector	% of sales by four largest firms	% of sales by foreign owned firms
France	1976	Basic chemicals	35	27
		Parachemicals*	18	48
		Pharmaceuticals	11	38
Germany	1976	Entire industry	32	23
UK	1976	Entire industry	28	23 (1973)

* Chemical products (other than pharmaceuticals) sold to final user.
Sources: France: STISI,[20,37] Germany: Deutsche[21] and Statistisches Bundesamt,[35] UK: Census of Production 1973 and 1976.

Table 2.5

Sales concentration and foreign participation in the iron and steel industry

Country	Year	% of sales by largest firms	% of sales by foreign owned firms
Germany	1977	3 firms : 35 6 firms : 54	40
France	1976	4 firms : 62	7

(The UK steel industry is mainly under state ownership; concentration ratios and data on foreign participation are not published.)

Sources: France : See Appendix II, page 96.
Germany : See Appendix II, page 101.

EEC as a whole in 1979, (Source : Eurostatistics, Commission of the European Communities). Three of the five largest steel producing companies in Europe have their headquarters in Germany. However, the major steel producing area comprises of the Ruhr and Rhein-Westfalen area of Germany, north-eastern France, southern and eastern Belgium, south-east Holland and Luxembourg. Firms such as Estel (Holland), ARBED (Luxembourg), Cockerill (Belgium) have major subsidiaries in West Germany. German based companies, (Thyssen, Mannesmann etc.), have manufacturing subsidiaries in Belgium and, on a smaller scale, in France.

Non-ferrous metal production is undertaken in EEC countries by firms based elsewhere in Europe (e.g. Alusuisse) or in North America (e.g. Alcan). The metal manufacturing industries are subject to government intervention and regulation in all countries, and the concentration ratios are of relatively little economic significance.

Mechanical engineering — agricultural engineering. Within mechanical engineering multinational operations are particularly significant in the production of agricultural machinery and civil engineering equipment. The proportions of sales attributable to foreign owned firms are much larger in this subsector than in other branches of non-electrical engineering, in all European countries for which data are available.

Reports published by the EEC Commission on the *agricultural engineering* industry cover three countries — West Germany (1972), the UK (1973), and France (1975). Trade between EEC countries in agricultural equipment and tractors has grown considerably since the abolition of tariff restrictions and there has been considerable, 'rationalisation of European operations', by some North American owned companies.

In Germany, certain big home based multinational companies, including Claas and Klockner-Humboldt-Deutz, produce alongside North American firms, with a high proportion of export sales. The proportion of sales attributable to foreign based firms and the concentration ratios are both reduced by this competitive structure.

The UK industry was dominated by four foreign owned firms and this is reflected by the figures in Table 2.6. Exports represented 52% of UK output in 1973 but imports accounted for 75% of the UK market. This high level of trade illustrates the policy of 'Europeanisation' on the part of North American companies.

The French agricultural equipment industry is less dominated by foreign capital than that of the UK, but the authors of the EEC Commission report for France pointed to the inability of domestic producers to respond to the big upsurge in demand for farm machinery in France, during the 1960s. This led to the loss of much of the market to foreign producers, (as in the UK), via imports and investment within France. Table

2.6 shows data on sales concentration and foreign participation in these three countries, up-dated as far as possible.

Table 2.6

Sales concentration and foreign participation in
agricultural engineering

Country	Year	% of sales obtained by 4 largest firms	% of sales obtained by foreign owned firms
France	1976	65	52
UK	1973	79	83
Germany	1972	37	23

Sources: France — STISI[27]

UK and Germany — EEC reports.

Electrical engineering — domestic appliances. It is difficult to split this broad sector because some major companies, (e.g. Siemens, Philips, GEC, ITT and Alsthom), are active in several branches. Some activities, such as the supply of equipment for generation and transmission tend to be the reserve of national companies within each EEC country. The basis of such reservation may be ordering by public authorities, or the design of technical barriers to imports of colour television transmission. The latter kind of protectionist measures can encourage investment by foreign companies in the country concerned. The degree of multinational operation is greatest in the supply of domestic electrical and electronic appliances.

Competition within Europe, in the case of domestic electrical appliances, (especially from Italy), and competition from elsewhere, (especially S.E. Asia), in the case of electronic equipment, has led to contraction and reorganisation of the European industries. Rationalisation and inter-company agreements have led to increased seller concentration during the 1970s. Table 2.7 shows sales concentration and foreign participation in selected countries in the latest years for which data are available. Table 2.8 shows changes in sales concentration between selected years, from various sources.

Some of the companies operating within the two sectors covered by Tables 2.7 and 2.8 are multinational undertakings with operations in both subsectors. The outstanding example is Philips, (of Holland). Other companies, while they have some multinational interests, are predominantly domestic suppliers of a wide range of products within each of the two sectors; e.g. the Thomson-Brandt group in France and the Thorn group in the UK. There are also more specialist firms which have tended to ex-

Table 2.7

Sales concentration and foreign participation in
domestic electrical and electronic appliances

Country	Year	% of sales by 4 largest firms	% of sales by foreign owned firms	Source
France	1976 A	38	18	STISI
	1976 B	34	37	STISI
Germany	1973 A	5	73	EEC
	1973 B	18	51	EEC
UK	1975 A	41	54	EEC
	1975 B	20	77	EEC
Italy	1973 A	15	62	EEC
	1973 B	*	45	EEC

A = Electrical appliances B = Electronic equipment
* Not available.

Table 2.8

Changes in sales concentration in domestic electrical goods

Country		No. of firms	Years and Combined shares (%)
France	A	4 firms	1972 : 32 1976 : 38
France	B	4 firms	1972 : 32 1976 : 34
Germany	A	4 firms	1968 : 48 1973 : 73
UK	A	5 firms	1968 : 48 1976 : 57
Italy	A	4 firms	1968 : 51 1970 : 62

A = Electrical appliances   B = Electronic equipment
(Data for 'B' for Germany, UK and Italy not comparable over sufficiently
long period.)

Sources: See various sources in Appendix II for France, Germany and
UK.
Italian data from reports of EEC Commission.

pand operations in other European countries: these include the French firm Moulinex, (electrical kitchen utensils), the Swedish Electrolux, (vacuum cleaners and refrigerators), and the Italian domestic appliance manufacturers Zanussi and Indesit, who have very recently acquired some former competitors in other countries.

In this industry an *oligopoly* appears to be emerging which embraces the entire EEC. National firms in individual countries have agreements with overseas suppliers, whereby they trade in each other's products, thus sharing the advantages of economies of scale in production, and national brand names. International negotiations between AEG in Germany and Zanussi in Italy have received some publicity and are described in Chapter 3. Most of the multinational operation shown in Tables 2.7 and 2.8 is from within Europe. There have been Japanese investments in the Irish Republic and more recently in Great Britain. Further reorganisation of the European industry to resist non-European competition seems likely.

Data processing equipment. The production of electronic computers is mainly dominated by large US companies. The International Business Machines Corporation, (IBM), was believed to hold 60% of the world market in 1978, with three other American companies — Honeywell, Univac and Burroughs — sharing a further 20%. In the growing markets for mini- and micro-computers, these companies are joined by other US producers such as DEC and Data General.[29]

IBM is the largest producer of computers, and associated equipment, in Europe. It has major production units in France, Germany, Italy and the UK, which were among the 60 largest industrial companies, (according to turnover), in each of these countries in 1979.[30] In each country the IBM subsidiary had a greater turnover from computing and office equipment than the largest domestic producer.

The production of 'Main Frame' computing systems is probably the activity which most strongly highlights the issues of multinational dominance. Economies of scale, (especially the recovery of research and development expenditures), create a tendency towards world oligopoly dominated by the US producers. Because the electronics industry is regarded as a sector important to economic growth and national security, some national governments have been reluctant to allow domestic computer companies to disappear or to fall completely under foreign control. For example, in the UK the Government assisted in the formation of ICL in the late 1960s, combining the computing interests of English Electric and ICT. ICL has been favoured by government purchasing preference, (as a declared policy until 1980), and received government assistance of £40 millions between 1972 and 1976. Although the state-owned National Enterprise Board sold its 25% holding of the equity of ICL in 1979, the UK government has during 1981 given a guarantee to potential creditors of up to £200 millions.[31]

In France, the major domestic producer, Compagnie des Machines Bull (CMB), ceded control of its computer manufacturing in 1964 by forming a joint subsidiary with the US firm General Electric (GE), in which GE had 66% of equity, and CMB had 34%. In 1970 GE's world-wide computer interests were sold to Honeywell Inc. and the French company was renamed Honeywell-Bull. In 1976, at the instigation of the French Government, Honeywell sold 19% of its holding in Honeywell-Bull to CMB. Honeywell-Bull merged at the same time with another, purely French computer group, Compagnie Internationale pour l'Informatique to form CII-Honeywell-Bull. Majority control of this new company was now in the hands of CMB, in which the French Government had a 20% stake. The French Government undertook to grant significant support to CII-Honeywell-Bull including annual subventions for the four years ended March 1980, based on deliveries to the French public sector. These subventions amounted to FF 1230 millions. During 1980 majority control of CMB, (51% of equity), was acquired by the French conglomerate and multinational St. Gobain Pont à Mousson (SGPM). This gave SGPM ultimate control of CII-Honeywell-Bull but nationalisation has been proposed during 1981.[32] The current ultimate parent of CII-Honeywell-Bull, Saint Gobain Pont à Mousson, has also acquired significant holdings in the major domestic producer of computers in Italy, Olivetti.[33]

Wider co-operation between Europe's computer manufacturers has also been urged publicly by ICL. Quoting support from the then President of the EEC Commission, the Chairman of ICL stated in his 1979 report that 'with the ending of national computer preference policies...', (under the EEC rules), '...ICL believes that the computer industry should be considered in a European context. ... The European computer market is currently dominated by companies based in the USA. If this dominance is not to go on increasing, there must be a Europe-wide strategy for maintaining a successful computer industry competence in the hardware, software and services sectors, with truly European ownership and control of the associated research and development facilities'.[34] The following year his successor has bemoaned the lack of progress in this direction.[35]

Motor vehicles. The motor industry attracted American capital before the Second World War, (in the UK, and again in the 1950s and 1960s. With the sale of Chrysler's subsidiaries in the UK and France to PSA-Peugeot Citröen, the French vehicle industry has now become almost entirely French owned (the truck production of Fiat is the only significant exception to this) and this, to some extent, results from French government policy in recent years. The Italian industry is dominated by

FIAT (partly state owned).

The two US companies (Ford and General Motors) operating in Germany and Britain both have component factories in France and assembly plants in Belgium, and Ford also has a tractor plant in Belgium and a truck assembly plant in Holland. These companies both operate increasingly on a European basis, in the same way as the manufacturers of agricultural machinery.

Economies of large scale production are one of the factors inducing national specialisation within the European operations of the major US vehicle companies. These economies occur not in the final assembly stage but in the manufacture of machined parts for engines and transmissions, and in the production of body panels and other metal pressings. Economies of scale, in production and in design and administration, also follow from 'rationalisation' of vehicle models — reduction in the number of models and the increased use of common components.

Because of economies of scale, the vehicle industries of Europe have become highly concentrated, with ratios in France, Germany and the UK as follows:

Germany (1975) $C_3\%$ = 51 (Monopolkomission)
France   (1976) $C_4\%$ = 57 (STISI)
UK   (1976) $C_5\%$ = 66 (Census of Production)

One issue which has recently received attention concerns the assembly of Japanese vehicles in Europe, within the EEC. The agreement between Honda and BL, whereby Honda designed cars will be produced in the UK, and the assembly of Japanese commercial vehicles in Ireland may be the beginning of an expanding Japanese assembly activity. It has already been pointed out that economies of scale in assembly are limited — by transferring assembly to a former export market a company can reduce the burden of tariffs and can possibly change its image within the new 'host country'.

Vehicle components — tyres. The production of certain components for motor vehicles tends to be very concentrated in most countries. The Commission of the European Communities has financed studies of the markets for batteries and sparking plugs in Germany, Italy and the UK, all of which have revealed high degrees of concentration. The statistical description of the supply of these two electrical components is however, incomplete, because some data on market shares could not be obtained by the research organisations.

A more detailed picture is available of concentration in the supply of tyres. The Commission's interest in this product was probably induced by the existence of an international oligopoly consisting mainly of US and European firms. There may have been concern in the Directorate

General for Competition about the continuing practice of dual pricing in the tyre industry. Under this practice, tyres are sold at low prices to vehicle producers for the 'original equipment' segment of the market, and at higher prices in the more captive replacement segment. Because tyres are a 'concern' product, (inferior tyres can cause death), the replacement market is believed to be more responsive to advertising than to price reductions.

The production of tyres is highly concentrated in all four countries listed in Table 2.9 – France, Germany, Italy and the UK. In each country the industrial structure is similar: one major domestic producer, (itself a multinational), plus subsidiaries of a small number of the foreign multinationals and finally some smaller firms serving only the national market and producing retreaded tyres or other specialist products.

Table 2.9

Sales concentration and foreign participation
in the supply of tyres

Country		Sales by 4 largest firms	Sales by foreign owned firms
France	(1974)	88	26
Germany	(1974)	72	50
Italy	(1974)	94	48
UK	(1975)	89	46

Source: EEC Commission reports

Financial links between major firms included that between Dunlop and Pirelli, whereby subsidiaries of each of the two companies were distributed between Dunlop Holdings and Pirelli Sp.A. on a 51-49 or 49-51 percentage basis. This financial near merger took place in 1970 but was not carried through to integration of marketing or management and during the late 1970s the two companies gradually reduced their interdependence, severing most of the remaining financial links in 1980.

Until 1980 the French firm Michelin had a 31% holding in the second largest French producer, Kléber-Colombes; these two firms together accounted for 74% of French production at the time of the survey in 1975, and for 70% of French domestic sales. The Austrian firm Semperit had the same parent company, (a Swiss finance group), as Kléber-Colombes. Financial difficulties of Kléber-Colombes, following the disposal of equity by the former majority holding company Semkler AG, led to a takeover by Michelin. This appears to put Michelin in a dominant position in the French market, (with a 70% market share). In Germany, the giant multinational chemicals firm Bayer A.G. has either majority or significant minority holdings in three tyre companies whose combined share of the German market is around 30%.

Foreign trade in tyres includes two elements. Some tyres are imported by firms with no manufacturing base in the importing country. However, there has been an increasing tendency for tyre producers with plants in two or more countries to transfer tyres between them, because this enables them to obtain more of the economies of long production runs on the one hand, and to reduce inventory costs on the other. The tyres industry has encountered a growing problem of excess capacity in recent years, with a slowing down of the growth of car ownership and with the large increase in tyre life brought about by product improvements, (a modern radial tyre has more than twice the life of a cross-ply tyre of ten years ago). In this situation, there has been price cutting, usually via short-term 'offers' by distributors, but financed by the producers. This is a sector where high concentration, on a world-wide scale, does not appear to have brought about the stability normally associated with this form of industrial structure.

Textiles. Historically, textile industries have developed in fragmented form, as the different requirements of each production stage discouraged vertical integration, and economies of scale in production are limited beyond a certain threshold size. The principal exception to this generalisation is the production of synthetic and cellulosic fibres which have replaced cotton, wool and flax in many of their former uses. This activity tends to be highly concentrated and includes some large, multinational chemicals producers. Forward integration by man-made fibre producers into textile processing activities has mainly been confined to the UK, where in the period 1963 — 68 Courtaulds and ICI acquired considerable textile interests. This process was stopped by the UK government which from 1970 has intervened to prevent further similar acquisitions. The forward integration, apparently stimulated by a desire on the part of the fibre producers to arrest the decline of the UK textile industry (their main customers), is reflected in much higher concentration ratios in the UK than elsewhere in the EEC.

The estimates in Table 2.10, based on various sources listed in Appendix II, show that in all three countries foreign participation was very low. This reflects the contraction in demand for textile products in developed countries — multinational expansion is generally associated with newer, expanding activities.

Table 2.10

Sales concentration and foreign participation
in textiles in 1976

Country	% of sales obtained by 4 largest firms	% of sales obtained by foreign owned firms
UK	31	5
France	8	6
Germany	5	7

Sources: See Appendix II

Conclusion. This analysis by sector has confirmed most of the expectations implied by earlier research, that foreign participation in national
industries is greatest in those sectors which are expanding, offer opportunities for exploitation of product improvements and mass marketing,
and where there are distinct advantages from local production, compared
with importing. In those industries where economies of large scale production are substantial and have long been enjoyed by local firms,
foreign participation is low. Our sectoral analysis has revealed a number
of cases where large multinational firms are now beginning to regard the
EEC as one area of operation, these are: agricultural machinery, certain
electrical goods, pharmaceuticals, (except in France), motor vehicles
and tyres.

High degrees of foreign participation and concentration coincide in
certain industries where the principal advantages of size are the ability
to finance research and development and investment in new products,
and/or to market products developed either in the host country or elsewhere. When economies of scale in production are low and advantages
of local production high, a high level of foreign participation may be
accompanied by low concentration. Finally, in some of the older industries there is very little foreign participation but domestic firms have
merged, or smaller firms have left the sector and there is a high degree
of concentration.

**Statistical analysis of the relationship between foreign participation and
concentration**

Analysis of the UK product data

One of the best known statistical studies of the relationship between
concentration and foreign participation is that directed by Max Steuer
and published in 1973.[36] This study used data from the UK Census of

Production for 1963, the latest then available, and showed conclusively that foreign investment and concentration tended to go together. Steuer extracted, for each product category for which the data were available, the proportion of total sales turnover, (domestic sales plus exports), obtained by the five largest enterprises, (C_5), and the combined share of subsidiaries of foreign owned firms. When all of 275 data pairs were included, he found that 15% of the variation in concentration was associated with foreign intervention and that this association was positive. Although this proportion is not large, it is too high to be attributed to chance, in view of the large sample size. When activities with zero foreign participation were excluded, the degree of association increased to 24%.* Steuer then went on to compare the increase in concentration in each product between the censuses of 1958 and 1963 with the degree of foreign participation. Did foreign participation increase or decrease concentration? The result of this comparison was that there was no net effect at all — the calculation indicated a slight negative relationship but this was so weak that it could be due to chance, (e.g. the way the products were defined).

In an earlier article on the same theme,[37] Steuer had pointed out that positive correlation between concentration and foreign participation was due to the absence of foreign firms in activities with low concentration. There were highly concentrated industries with little foreign participation. We repeated Steuer's analysis of product concentration in the UK with data from the 1968 Census of Production, the last such census to contain detailed information about foreign participation. Our results were almost identical with those of Steuer: with 244 comparable pairs of data the correlation coefficient was found to be 0.33; when 75 groups with foreign participation equal to zero were excluded, the coefficient rose to 0.40. These values were much too high to be attributed to chance. In order to test Steuer's thesis that positive correlation was due to the small number of activities with high foreign participation but with low concentration, we grouped the products according to whether a share of sales gained by foreign owned firms was above or below 30%, and whether the five firm concentration ratio was above or below 65%, (approximately the mean level). Table 2.11 shows the results, which strongly support Steuer's thesis.

---

* The proportions quoted are the squares of the linear correlation coefficients, r^2 (r_2), between the two variables, (concentration and foreign participation). This statistic is derived by examining deviations of one, (dependent), variable from its average value and measuring what proportion of the sum of the squares of these deviations can be explained by a, (linear), relationship with the other variable.

Table 2.11

Product concentration and share of sales achieved by
foreign controlled companies — UK 1968

Foreign share	Five firm concentration ratio	
	Below 65%	Above 65%
Zero	39	36
1 to 30%	70	55
Above 30%	9	35
	118	126

(See Appendix II for Chi-squared test which shows that this result is too pronounced to be due to chance in choice of sample.)

Source: Compiled data from the 1968 Census of Production

We then applied the same test as Steuer to compare the changes in concentration between the two years (1963 and 1968) with the level of concentration. Our results showed a *significant* negative correlation (unlike those of Steuer for 1958 to 1963). In other words, concentration tended to increase more in the product groups with less foreign participation and this tendency, (though fairly weak), was too widespread to be attributed to chance. This result may be misleading. First, foreign participation tended to be at a higher level in more concentrated industries. The greater the existing level of concentration, the less the scope for concentration to increase. Secondly, foreign companies were more strongly represented in expanding activities, and increases in concentration are more usually associated with declining sectors. There are two reasons for this: (a) new firms join expanding activities and existing firms leave declining ones, (b) 'rationalisation', often encouraged by governments, (as in Britain between 1963 and 1968), is usually introduced in declining activities.

In Appendix II, we show that in the UK for the periods 1963 — 68 and 1968 — 75, changes in product concentration were negatively, (significantly), related to changes in sales and to concentration levels at the beginning of each period. Foreign participation does not appear to have had additional influence on changes in concentration, once allowance has been made for these other two factors. No significant correlation was found between changes in concentration and changes in foreign participation in different product groups. This result underlines the indirect nature of the negative relationship between changes in concentration and the level of participation, described in the preceding paragraphs.

Concentration ratios for product groups relate to the total supply of the products from all sources within the country. Much more information, (for the UK and certain other European countries), is available for groups of establishments classified as 'industries' or 'sectors' on the basis of their principal product. The data on those establishments under the ownership, (majority control), or a single enterprise are then grouped to provide an 'enterprise' analysis.

Hart and Clarke[38] have recently published a comprehensive study of the data from the UK Census of Production. They showed that over 78% of the variance* in estimated five firm concentration ratios of 141 industries, could be explained by three independent variables: the average number of plants per enterprise in the industry, the median plant size, (for Florence median — see Appendix II), and total employment in the industry. The first two variables had a positive effect on concentration, the third had a negative effect. The negative effect of total size can best be understood when considered alongside the two other variables. For any given average plant size and given number of plants per enterprise, the number of enterprises in an industry will be determined by the industry's total size. We have refined some of the measurements used by Hart and Clarke, and still using their specification, have been able to raise the proportion of the variance explained, (R^2), to nearly 84%. We have also examined whether the inclusion of foreign participation, (measured by a weighted average of product participation rates), adds to this explained variance ratio. Our conclusion, (shown mathematically in Appendix II), is negative: foreign involvement in an industry has no significant effect on concentration once allowance has been made for the three factors identified by Hart and Clarke.

The simple correlation between foreign participation and concentration was 0.225 for 110 industries for which pairs of data were available. When the 25 industries with zero foreign participation were excluded this coefficient rose to 0.36 — both these values were significantly different from zero. This finding is consistent with that described in the preceding paragraph, because a significant part of inter-industry variation in the foreign participation is explained by the three factors which explain most of the variations in concentration. Excluding those industries with no foreign involvement (often for political reasons), we found 27% of variance in the share of sales by foreign firms explained by the three variables: average plants per enterprise, (negative effect), median plant size (positive effect) and size of the industry, (negative effect). Each of the three variables was statistically significant. The addition of

---

* This figure is the square of the multiple correlation coefficient (R^2)

46

the concentration ratio as an additional variable in this equation had a negligible effect.

The results of this statistical examination of these influences on foreign participation in industries in the UK are consistent with expectations. Multinationals are not generally associated with activities in which the plant size is small: investment in many small plants overseas might create management and communication difficulties. This explains why foreign participation in each industry is correlated positively with median plant size, and negatively with the plants per enterprise ratio. The negative correlation with the size of the industry is probably a result of definition – one possible reason is the use of employment as the size variable. As shown in Chapter 3, foreign owned companies are generally in less labour intensive activities, and have higher sales per employee ratios than domestically based companies.

Although median plant size, the plants per enterprise ratio and the size of the industry appear to account for the correlation between foreign involvement and concentration in the UK, they do not explain much of the inter-industry variation in foreign participation. This negative conclusion reinforces some of the work of Caves, Dunning and others, (see bibliography), – other variables need to be added into the explanation of foreign investment in a host country. Our analysis suggests that these may not be correlated with sales concentration.

For example, advertising expenditure as a proportion of sales is positively correlated with foreign participation in sales. Only 40 pairs of observations were available from the 1968 Census industry data, because either of the two variables was missing for the other 103 industries included in the Census. The correlation coefficient between advertising as a percentage of sales and foreign participation was 0.47% which, while less than expected, was significantly different from zero. There was almost zero correlation between the advertising to sales ratio and concentration. Experience in advertising and marketing is one of the intangible assets which, according to Caves, Dunning and others quoted earlier in this chapter, multinational operation is designed to exploit.

French data

French data on concentration and foreign participation are comprehensive but have been published only for very recent years. Comparisons of levels of concentration at both product, ('branche') and industry, ('secteur') level in 1975 and 1976 are presented in Appendix II and summarised as follows. A comparative analysis for 1972 also produced interesting results.

Product concentration　Although data on foreign subsidiaries' shares of sales of individual products were not available, the French statistics on product concentration list, (in order), the four largest producers of each of the 282 product groups.[23] By identifying the subsidiaries of non-French companies and constructing an index of 'the importance of foreign firms', we were able to show a very weak but statistically significant positive correlation between foreign penetration and concentration. As in the UK this correlation was due to the relatively small number of cases where concentration was low and foreign participation high. The analysis in Appendix II shows that considerable manipulation of the data was required before any statistically significant results could be obtained — the relationship is much less pronounced than in the UK. There are more cases of high foreign penetration and low concentration, some of which were described earlier in this chapter.

Industry concentration. The French statistics on foreign participation include information on minority holdings and an 'Index of foreign penetration', (*indice de pénétration étrangère*). This adds to the share of industry sales, (employment or another variable), gained by majority owned subsidiaries, a proportion of the sales etc. of each company of which a single foreign shareholder owns between 20 and 50%. The relationships between this index and various concentration indices[25] are significant both for sales and employment. Figures A2.1 to A2.4 at the end of Appendix II show distributions of the pairs of observations for 34 industries — it can be seen that there are few industries in which foreign penetration is high and concentration low. The correlation at industry level between foreign penetration and concentration is higher than that observed in the UK from 1968 data. The correlation coefficient between the four firm concentration ratio for employment in France and foreign penetration was 0.48 compared with the UK figure of 0.23. When more sophisticated concentration indices were used and sales taken as the variable studied, even higher correlations were derived from the French data.

In order to include data on plant sizes in the French analysis, we took employment concentration in 1972.[25] We found that over 80% of the variance, (a multiple correlation of about 0.9), in the four firm concentration ratio could be explained by a model incorporating economies of scale and foreign penetration. (Economies of scale were represented by the proportion of employment in the industry which was in establishments with 500 or more employees.) The results showed that foreign penetration of an industry was significantly correlated with concentration even after allowance had been made for economies of scale, to which both concentration and foreign penetration were linked. Comparison of the *changes* in concentration levels between 1972 and 1976 in 33 industrial sectors with the corresponding levels of foreign participation, revealed virtually zero correlation. Changes in concentration were generally small over this period. Revision of the industrial classification for most data, (other than concentration ratios), prevented further statistical analysis to investigate this absence of correlation.

German data

Concentration ratios for industries in the German Federal Republic were published for the first time for 1977.[26] Data for foreign participation in broad industry groups have so far been published only for 1976 and 1977.[20] These data are based on classification of enterprises by their principal product, so that there may be some distortion compared with the use of data based on establishments.

The Deutsche Bundesbank has supplied us with data on foreign participation in each of 27 manufacturing sectors in Germany in 1977 and 1978, also based on classification of enterprises. The 1977 data may be compared with the industrial census results for the same year.[28] Figure A2.5 at the end of Appendix II shows that there was a fairly high degree of correlation between the proportion of sales achieved by foreign controlled firms and the six firm sales concentration ratio, ($r=0.75$).* Figure A2.6 shows a similar correlation in the case of employment. In each case the correlation was due mainly to the absence of foreign owned firms from industries with low concentration, a finding which is consistent with the evidence for the UK and France. The German evidence is very striking, as shown in Table 2.12.

Table 2.12*

Foreign participation and sales concentration in
27 German manufacturing sectors

Share of sales turnover obtained by foreign controlled firms (%)	Six firm sales concentration (%)	
	Below 30	Above 30
Below 20	13	5
Above 20	1	8
	14	13

Source: The Deutsche Bundesbank

* See Appendix II for definition of the foreign controlled firm. It should be noted that the 'enterprise' as defined in the German Statistical Office data, does not include subsidiaries with separate legal identity. This means that German concentration ratios understate concentration compared with those for France and the UK, where financial control, (rather than legal identity), is the criterion for definition.

Further analysis of the German data showed that three variables explained much of the inter-industry variation in concentration levels: the average number of employees per establishment, the ratio of plants per enterprise, and total employment in the industry. (The choice of these variables followed the research of Hart and Clarke in the UK.) These three variables explained 66% of inter-industry variance of sales concentration and 68% of employment concentration in Germany, in 1977. The inclusion of foreign participation as an additional variable in these two statistical analyses did not increase these proportions significantly. The similarity between these research findings and those for the UK in 1968 is evident. It is interesting to note that the much closer correlation in Germany between concentration and foreign participation can be explained by the closer relationship between foreign participation and the same three factors. They accounted for about 66% of inter-industry variation in foreign participation in sales, and 69% of that in employment. An unexpected finding was a positive correlation between foreign participation and the plant enterprise ratio. The reasons for this and the contrast with the finding for the UK cannot be identified without more detailed research, beyond the objectives of this study.

International comparison and conclusions

In all three countries for which we have analysed available data, there is statistically significant correlation between the level of concentration in each industry, and the degree of foreign participation. The correlation is strongest in Germany. In all three countries, the correlation was due mainly to the absence of industrial sectors, (or product groups), in which concentration was low but foreign participation high. We showed that inter-industry differences in concentration in the UK and Germany could largely be explained by economies of scale, the plants per enterprise ratio, and the size of the industry; (generally, the smaller the defined activity the greater the concentration). Since foreign participation was significantly influenced by these same three variables, the correlation with concentration could be explained. Once allowance had been made for their influence, there was no additional statistical link between concentration and foreign penetration, in either Germany or the UK. Economies of scale, (the proportion of employees in establishments with 500 or more), also explain much of the inter-industry variation in concentration levels in France.Once allowance has been made for this factor — the residual correlation between industry concentration and foreign penetration is weak.

Since it appears that the correlation between foreign participation and concentration in all three countries can be substantially explained away by other variables, it is necessary to study changes in the two variables to identify any causal connection. In the UK with product-group data, there was virtually zero statistical connection between changes in foreign participation and changes in concentration. There was a negative correlation between the *level* of participation and changes in concentration, but this became insignificant when allowance was made for change in sales over the periods studied, (1963 – 68 and 1968 – 75), and for the initial concentration level. Foreign participation was not generally associated with declining industries, in which concentration tended to increase. In France there was virtually zero correlation between changes in concentration and the level of foreign participation.

The conclusion of this statistical section is that in France and the UK, a positive relationship between foreign participation and concentration results mainly from the absence of foreign investment in low concentrated industries and product markets. This relationship is weak and not causal – it reflects mainly the need for a minimum economic scale to justify investment in a foreign country. In West Germany, the relationship is stronger but further analysis again revealed that it could be explained by other, possibly incidental, variables. Until data for Germany are available for a longer period and changes in concentration and foreign participation can be compared, it will not be possible to determine whether there is any *causal* relationship between the operation of foreign owned subsidiaries and business concentration.

Notes

1   See: Madeuf, B.,'Peut-on definir les multinationales' in *Les Multinationales*, Cahiers Français no. 190, la Documentation Française, Paris, 1979, pp. 2–3.

2   See: Vernon R., *Multinational Companies and National Sovereignty*, Harvard Business Review, March–April 1967, pp. 156–72.

3   See: Michalet, C.F., *Le capitalisme mondial*, Presse Universitaire Francaise, Paris, 1976, p. 16.

4   See: Vernon R., *Sovereignty at Bay – The Multinational Spread of US Enterprises*, Longman, Harlow, 1971.

5   See: Michalet, C.F.,'Les Bmn: nouvelle vague des multinationales' in: op. cit reference 1, (above).

6   See: US Department of Commerce, *Survey of Current Business*, Washington, September 1973 and March 1978.

7   See: Caves, R.E., 'Industrial Organisation' in Dunning J.H. (ed.), *Economic Analysis and the Multinational Enterprise*, Allen and Unwin, London, 1974; and Caves, R.E. *Cause of Direct Investment: Foreign Firms' Shares in Canadian and United Kingdom Manufacturing Industries*, Review of Economics and Statistics, Vol. 56, London, 1974.

8 See: Vaupel, J.W., *Characteristics and Motivation of US Companies which invest abroad*, Harvard University mimeograph, 1971.

9 See: Michalet, C.F., 'Pourquoi des firms multinationales?' in: op cit reference 1 (above).

10 See: Franko, L.G., *The European Multinationals*, Harper and Row, London, 1971.

11 See: Ghertman, M. and Siegmund, M., *Danone avec Fruits*, Centre d'Enseignement Superieur des Affaires, Jouy-en-Joses, France, 1973.

12 See: Safarian, A.E., *The Performance of US Firms in Canada*, Canadian-American Committee, Toronto, 1969.

13 See: Knickerbocker, F.T., *Oligopolistic Reaction and Multinational Enterprise*, Harvard Business School, 1973.

14 See: Dunning, J.H., 'Multinational Enterprises, Market Structure, Economic Power and Industrial Policy'. *Journal of World Trade Law*, Twickenham, 1974.

15 See: Van den Bulcke, D., *Les entreprises étrangères dans l'industrie belge*, University of Gent, 1971. (*De buitenlandse onderningen in de belgische industrie*, Seminaire voor toegpaste economie, Rijkuniversitet Gent.)

16 Source: Commission of the European Communities, *First Report on Competition Policy*, Brussels, 1972, p. 159. (Available in all Community languages.)

17 See: OECD, *Penetration of Multinational Firms in the Manufacturing Industry of Member Countries*, (*Pénétration de Firmes Multinationales dans l'Industrie Manufacturière des Pays-Membres*), Paris, 1979.

18 Source: Van den Bulcke, D., 'The motives for disinvestment from EEC countries' in *Investment and Divestment Policy of Multinational Corporations in Europe*, 'Les motifs de désinvestissement dans les pays de la CEE' in *'Politiques d'investissement, reductions ou cessations d'activité de multinationales en Europe'*, ECSIM, Brussels, 1979, p. 23.

19 Source: Service du Traitement de l'Information et des Statistiques Industrielles (STISI), *L'Implantation Etrangère dans l'Industrie au 1er janvier 1978*. Documentation Française, Paris, 1980 (published for each year from 1975).

20 Source: *Commission of the European Communities*: Concentration series reports quoted are published only in the language in which they were written. General title is 'A Study of the Evolution of Concentration in the (industry) in (country)'.

21 Source: Deutsche Bundesbank, *The level of direct investment at the end of 1977*, Monthly Report of the DB, Vol. 32, No 4, Frankfurt,

April 1980, (available in English and original German.)

22　See: Marfels, C., *A Study on Evolution of Concentration in the Food Industry of the Federal Republic of Germany*, Commission of the European Communities, Brussels, 1980.

23　See: UK Business Statistics Office, *Statistics of Product Concentration of UK Manufacturers in 1963, 1968 and 1975*, Business Monitor PQ 1006, London, 1979.

24　See: Brocard, R., *Les entreprises françaises: Concentration et grandes entreprises des secteurs et des branches,* INSEE (Ref. E64), Paris, 1979, p. 134.

25　Source: Nouvel Economiste, *Classement 1979 des Premières Sociétés Françaises et Européennes*, Paris, 1979.

26　See: Monopolies Commission, *The Supply of Chlordiazepoxide and Diazepam*, HMSO, London, 1973.

27　See: STISI (see ref. 19), *La Concentration des Entreprises Industrielles de 1972 à 1976*, (Recueils Statistiques no. 13), Documentation Française, Paris 1979.

28　See: Statistisches Bundesamt, '*Beschaftigung Umsatz und Investitionen der Unternehmen in Bergbau und in Verarbeitenden Gewerbe*' (Reihe 4, 2, 1), Wiesbaden 1980.

29　See: UK National Economic Development Office, Electronic Computers SWP, *The role of foreign owned multinational companies in the UK computing industry*, NEDO, London, 1979, p. 2.

30　See: *Europe's 5000 Largest Companies*, Dun and Bradstreet, London, 1981, pages 299, 305, 308 and 311.

31　Source: ICL, *Annual Reports*, 1975–80.

32　Sources: CII-Honeywell-Bull, *Annual Reports*, 1976–80, (and also reports in the *Financial Times*.)

33　Source: Olivetti, *Annual Report*, May 1980.

34　Source: Chairman of ICL, *Annual Report 1979*, p. 6.

35　See: ICL, *Annual Report 1980*, p. 6.

36　See: Steuer, M., 'Monopoly Power and the inward investing firm' in Steuer et al., *The Impact of Foreign Direct Investment in the UK*, HMSO, London, 1973.

37　See: Steuer, M, 'Competition and the Multinational firm: the United Kingdom case' in J.B. Heath, (ed.), *Proceedings of International conferences on monopolies, mergers and restrictive practices 1969*, HMSO, London, 1971.

38   See: Hart, P.E. and Clarke, R., *Concentration in British Industry 1935–75*, National Institute Occasional Paper, National Institute of Economic and Social Research, London, 1980.

3 Characteristics and behaviour of multinational firms in concentrated industries

The distinctive features of multinational firms

Foreign subsidiaries have certain distinctive characteristics which influence their business and competitive strategies. Data from individual European countries shows that subsidiaries of foreign companies located in those countries differ from home based firms in the following respects:

1 They tend to undertake only part of the total manufacturing process; they include fewer 'vertically integrated' operations.

2 Partly because of 1 (above) they tend to operate comparatively few small plants.

3 They are generally more productive, in terms of value added per employee, probably because they are more capital intensive.

4 They tend to pay higher wages and salaries than domestically based companies.

In this section we present evidence on these four distinct differences.

Subsidiaries of foreign companies are less vertically integrated

Statistical evidence on this distinctive feature is available for the UK and for France.[1&2]* In the UK the ratio of the total value added to the total sales of foreign owned companies in manufacturing industry in

* See page 75 for notes.

1977 was 30.2%. The corresponding ratio for the domestic operations of UK companies was 35.0%.[1] The Census of Production gives separate information for each of the 15 broad sectors of manufacturing industry and it was possible to check whether *in each sector* foreign owned companies had less vertical integration than their UK owned counterparts. This analysis showed that in only 2 of the 15 sectors, (basic fuels and timber products), was the ratio of value added to sales for foreign owned firms greater than the average for the sector. We then tested whether foreign owned companies had less value added in relation to sales purely because of their predominance in less vertically integrated sectors. The statistical results described in Appendix II confirm that this is very improbable — the results suggest that, on average, foreign firms spent a greater amount on purchases per unit of sales, than domestic firms in the same sector.

Evidence for *France* yields a similar conclusion. In 1977 majority controlled foreign subsidiaries in France had a value added to sales ratio of 25.6%, while for companies with less than 20% foreign capital the corresponding figure was 35.1%.[2] The Index of Foreign Penetration, (IPE), which is defined in Appendix II and is a percentage measure of the importance of foreign owned companies, was calculated at 20.2% for sales, and only 15.7% for value added. As with the UK data, it was possible to make this comparison in each sector: the French statistics in 1977 were analysed for 36 manufacturing sectors. In only 6 of these was the index of foreign penetration of value added greater than that of sales. The 6 sectors were iron and steel, non-ferrous metals, glass, data processing equipment, electrical generating machinery and motor vehicle production. In all of these cases, the value added penetration was only *very slightly* greater than that of sales. A statistical analysis, also described in Appendix II shows that, on average, foreign firms have a lower ratio of value added to sales than home based firms in the same sector.

The similar conclusions of the analysis for the UK and that for France correspond with the predictions of earlier researchers and authors on this subject. Most multinational operation within Europe consists of 'horizontal' investments. The establishment and development of the European Common Market was expected to encourage this process — the Europeanisation of activities so that companies could 'rationalise' operations on a horizontal basis, to obtain economies of scale through international division of production.

Foreign owned companies operate fewer small establishments (plants)

This observation follows from the discussion of the predominance of large scale 'horizontal' investment discussed in the previous paragraph.

In the UK in 1977 the average size of the foreign owned establishment was 256 employees, while that of the UK owned establishment was 43 employees.[1] The corresponding figures for France show foreign owned, (majority controlled), establishments with an average of 156 employees, French owned, (ie. less than 20% foreign), with a corresponding average of 105 employees.[2] The French data exclude enterprises with fewer than 20 employees. When allowance is made for this difference the results are fairly similar, and occur because few small production establishments, (fewer than 100 employees), are owned by foreign firms in either of the two countries.

These results for the UK and France were also expected, from previously published research. Data for Germany were not available.

Foreign companies have higher labour productivity

Because of the lower degrees of vertical integration, it is invalid to compare sales per employee in foreign owned and domestically owned companies. This objection prevents the use of the large volume of data available for such comparison in several European countries.

The 1977 Census of Production for the *UK*[1] confirms that *value added* per employee in foreign owned subsidiaries is, on average, higher than in domestic firms. This difference has been observed over a number of years. The 1977 data shows that in the manufacturing industry as a whole, the average value added per employee in foreign owned firms was 43% greater than the corresponding average for domestic firms. A check of 15 industrial sectors showed that in only 2 was the average value added per employee in foreign firms lower than that of UK based companies. A statistical test based on the sectoral data confirmed that the higher average productivity of foreign firms could not be explained by their distribution among the 15 sectors. (See Appendix II.)

Data for *France* in 1977[2] again shows a similar situation to that in the UK, though the difference is much less pronounced — foreign subsidiaries in manufacturing achieved, on average, 14% more value added per employee than their French owner counterparts. Sectoral comparison, (based on the index of foreign penetration), revealed that in 27 of the 36 sectors, value added per employee was higher in foreign owned than in French companies. Statistical analysis of the sectoral data showed it very unlikely that the higher average productivity of foreign firms could be explained by their distribution among the 36 sectors.

The UK and French findings are supported by data for *Belgium* in 1968, presented by Van den Bulcke.[3] Value added per employee in foreign owned companies exceeded that of domestic firms in each of seven broad groupings of manufacturing industry. None of these findings is unexpected. Writers quoted earlier, (and also later in this chapter), have postulated that multinational operation will generally be associated with technically advanced capital intensive activities. For none of the three countries in which we have compared productivity levels are there any data on *capital per employee*. For this, it is necessary to make an indirect comparison with the German Federal Republic. German data for the end of 1976[4] show that in foreign companies, (i.e. where at least 25% of capital is held by one foreign shareholder), net assets per employee are 48% greater than in other companies in manufacturing. Comparison in 14 broad sectors of German industry shows capital per employee is greater in foreign firms, except in *1* sector, (food, drink and tobacco), where German firms have greater capital intensity and another, (wood processing), where the ratios are almost identical.

Data on capital productivity would be useful in comparison of efficiency but these are not available for any of the countries surveyed. Comparisons of returns on capital are of doubtful validity because profit performance of subsidiaries can be significantly distorted by international transfers. (Transfer pricing is discussed in the previous section).

Subsidiaries of foreign companies pay higher wages

There are two ways in which the multinationality of firms might, (in principle), affect negotiations in the labour market. First, they might be able to use their multinational operations and ability to switch production as a bargaining strength — their ability to withstand disputes might be increased because of this ability. The strength of this argument is weakened by collaboration between trade unions both nationally and internationally. An example of national collaboration is the usual refusal of dockers to handle imports by multinationals, of products from factories in other countries intended to replace production hindered by strikes or other disputes. An example of the second kind occurred when Ford workers in Germany refused to increase production during the 1978 strike in the UK.

The second possible effect of multinationality on wage negotiations operates to push wages upwards. Employees compare wages paid by the multinational employer in all countries, and unions tend to demand international parity. Since parity with the highest wages in the industry in each individual country is another element in wage demands, this theory would predict a continuing ratchet effect on the wage rates of multinationals, causing these to be higher, at any one time, than those of domestic firms. Multinationals may also be able to afford to pay more, and be more vulnerable to industrial disputes. It has been shown that they tend to have greater labour productivity and also that they are more capital intensive. The generally lower level of vertical integration may be another influence. In a vertically integrated firm, management has to consider the implications for earlier and subsequent processes of pay concessions at any particular stage. Evidence from the UK, France and Belgium suggests that in all three countries wage and salary levels are higher in the subsidiaries of foreign companies, than in home based firms. The UK evidence is again from 1977 Census of Production.[1] This shows that average total remuneration per employee was 14.7% greater in foreign owned companies than in other companies. (This is much less than the difference in productivity of 43%, described in the previous subsection on 'Foreign companies have higher labour productivity'.)

For further investigation, the data were divided in two ways: we separated analyses for 'operatives', and 'clerical, technical and administrative staff', (as given in the Census); the sectoral data were also examined, for each group of employees. It is interesting to note a higher proportion of employees of foreign owned companies fell into the category 'clerical, technical and administrative staff' — 33% compared with 27% in domestic firms. A greater proportion of such staff in foreign subsidiaries was found in 13 of the 15 sectors into which manufacturing industry was divided. This finding was a little surprising — such staff are normally associated with head office activities. It may be partly explained by the higher productivity of operatives in foreign owned firms — there has until recently been much greater scope for increases in productivity in manual work. Another factor may be the greater importance to foreign owned subsidiaries of the marketing and research functions (discussed in section in the next section.)

In 1977 manual workers, ('operatives'), in foreign manufacturing subsidiaries in the UK received average earnings which were 13.9% greater than those employed by other manufacturing companies. An analysis by broad industrial sectors showed that manual employees of foreign owned firms had higher earnings in 13 of 15 sectors. Statistical analysis confirmed that the higher overall average for foreign owned companies cannot be explained by the distribution of such firms among the 15 sectors. The comparison for non-manual workers, ('clerical, technical and administrative staff'), revealed similar results. The average salary of such employees in foreign owned companies was 11.5% above the corresponding figure for other manufacturers. Non-manual employees of foreign owned firms had higher earnings in 14 of the 15 sectors, and statistical analysis again confirmed that the overall result is not due to distribution among these 15 sectors. The comparison for non-manual, ('clerical, technical and administrative staff'), revealed similar results. The average salary of such employees in foreign owned companies was 11.5% above the corresponding figures for other manufacturers. Non-manual employees of foreign owned firms had higher earnings in 14 of the 15 sectors, and statistical analysis again confirmed that the overall result is not due to distribution among these 15 sectors.

Data for *France* reinforce the conclusions based on UK data. In 1977 the average earnings of employees in foreign controlled subsidiaries in French industry were 12.5% above those in French owned firms. In 29 out of 35 industrial sectors, employees in foreign controlled firms received average earnings greater than the corresponding average in French owned enterprises. A statistical analysis of the sectoral data showed that the observation of foreign firms paying higher wages could not be explained by the distribution of those firms among the 35 sectors. Van den Bulcke reports a similar comparison of wages in foreign owned and domestic firms in each of the 15 sectors of manufacturing industry in *Belgium*, in 1968.[3] The average rate per hour was higher in foreign owned companies in 14 of the 15 sectors.

Business and competitive strategies of multinational firms

The advantages and disadvantages of multinational subsidiaries compared with single country firms

Advantages. In Chapter 1 we suggested that the advantages of multinational firms, (both in their home countries and abroad), were due partly to their geographical diversification and partly to their size. Their geographical diversification increases options open to companies in a number of situations. For example, differential pricing enables them to take advantage of different price sensitivities in the various national markets within which they operate. This will increase total sales revenue from any given volume of goods produced. Greater opportunity for differential pricing is available to the company producing in different countries, than the firm which is supplying them by exports. This is because the multinational is in each country operating within any protective barriers, (either fiscal or in terms of consumer loyalty). Where such barriers do not exist, the multinational has no advantage in this respect. One feature, which has become apparent in the EEC with the abolition of many trade restrictions, is the ability of multinational firms to move goods between national markets. By producing within a country the company becomes known as a domestic firm and is able to avoid any national antipathy towards imports. For example, the multinational motor companies transfer vehicles within Europe to take advantage of differing market conditions and availability of inventories. Whereas purchases by companies, (as opposed to private purchases), in the UK include very few cars which are immediately recognised as non-British, cars imported from EEC plants by Ford, General Motors, (Vauxhall), and British Leyland are accepted. Another advantage of diversification is the spreading of risk, and the ability to adjust to adverse conditions, unless these coincide in all the markets served by the company. Such conditions may include recessions in demand, shortages of components or other supplies and labour disputes, (though in some cases the company's freedom of action may be limited by international co-operation among trade unions).

60

The sheer size of its global operations enables a multinational to achieve economies of scale in research and product development, publicity, (on a world wide scale), and the raising of finance. These advantages of size reinforce those arising from the geographical diversity of its operations. The enterprise with subsidiary companies in several countries may also be able to increase its after tax profits by manipulation of transfer prices between these companies. Examples of this possible advantage and limitations to it are discussed separately in the next subsection, under the paragraph heading 'Transfer pricing'.

Disadvantages. Some competitive disadvantages may be encountered by the multinational firm in foreign countries. Physical remoteness from the head office may restrict the independence of local management and the speed of reaction to sudden change. Improved communications, including multiple access computing facilities using telecommunications satellites, have reduced the importance of physical distance. Discussions about such systems suggest that they encourage greater standardisation in the way decisions are taken. This might reduce adaptation to local conditions. When the senior executives of foreign companies are expatriates from the home country, they may tend to stand aside from some of the informal networks of business communication in the host country. They may also be at a disadvantage compared with nationals because of less understanding of social or cultural norms. For example, the design of shift systems for employees needs to allow for regional traditions; we found in earlier research[5] that multinational companies had experienced greater problems through shift arrangements, than nationally based firms with greater local knowledge.

Although the foreign owned subsidiary has distinct trading advantages over the foreign firm supplying a national market by exports, it may not be as favourably regarded as its domestic competitors by customers with a 'nationalistic' bias. This is particularly true of public purchases: the political pressure to buy at home also extends to purchasing from home based firms. Both the UK and French governments have explicitly pursued policies of preference for domestic purchasing of computer equipment, until 1980. Since then, both governments have continuing financial involvement with domestic producers, (see Chapter 2). Governments may also discriminate in the awarding of discretionary assistance, in favour of companies generating most employment (indirectly as well as directly) within the host country.

The competitive strategies of multinationals

Advertising. In Chapter 2 we explained that previous research had shown that many multinational operations are undertaken in industries with high rates of expenditure on marketing, (e.g. advertising, sales promotion, multiple branding). Many writers have associated multi-national companies in Europe with massive consumer advertising, and point out that these firms dominate the advertising media — especially in the case of press and commercial television. A survey of leading advertisers in continental Europe, published in 1979[6] covered France, Germany, Italy, Spain, Belgium, the Netherlands, Norway and Sweden. Six companies, (Unilever, Procter and Gamble, Colgate-Palmolive, Nestle, General Motors and Philips), were among the top 15 company advertisers in at least four of these eight countries. In Germany, 5 of the 6 largest advertisers were foreign multinationals and the remaining German firm, (Henkel), was among leading advertisers elsewhere in Europe. In the UK, in 1976 there were 38 manufacturing companies among the top 50 firms ranked according to total expenditure on press and TV advertising.[7] The combined expenditure of these 38 companies accounted for 71% of all expenditure on consumer advertising of manufactured goods. Of the 38, 25 were British based firms and 12 foreign owned; the other company Unilever, which is part British and part Dutch, was the largest single advertiser with over 5% of the total.

The high rate of advertising expenditure by multinational companies can be explained by their predominance in industries characterised by high advertising expenditure. We undertook an analysis of shares of domestic sales and of advertising expenditure during the four year period 1974 — 77 in two sectors of the UK domestic market with high rates of advertising — foods and domestic electrical appliances. In no case was the combined share of advertising by foreign owned firms within an individual product market significantly different from their combined share of sales. Within these markets there is no evidence to suggest that foreign owned firms devote a significantly greater proportion of sales income to advertising.

The method used to determine the expected level of advertising in relation to sales was a calculation of the statistical relationship between the share of advertising and the share of sales, (see Appendix II, p. 105—6). The results suggest that may be due to economies of scale in advertising, since the ratio of advertising to sales *within the same product sectors*, decreases with the market share of the firm. They also indicate that the scale of advertising by foreign owned subsidiaries, was very similar to that of UK based firms of similar size in the same activities. This evidence suggests that fears of advertising increasing, as industries become both more concentrated and dominated by multinationals, may be misplaced.

Product innovation. This is one of the most important competitive weapons used by multinationals. It reflects their size and ability to finance research and also their geographical diversity — new products

62

can be tested in different markets and refinements and selections made. One of the long-standing theories about the reasons for multinational operation is that first described by Vernon in 1966[8] — the product life cycle model. (This is summarised and assessed by Hood and Young[9].) This theory asserts that a firm is most likely to expand output abroad when the demand for a product in its home country has reached its peak and, by implication, latent demand in the countries of overseas operations has not been realised. Evidence from studies of European and US firms[9] shows that in both areas of the world, multinational firms devote a higher proportion of sales to research and development, than firms with limited or aero international production. Does this comparatively high rate of expenditure on research and development occur at the level of the foreign subsidiary, or is the high technology work centralised in the home country? Research by Dunning[10] suggests that UK subsidiaries of US firms spend a greater proportion of sales on research and development than UK based firms. However, like the advertising intensity relationship, this last finding may reflect a bias towards research intensity in the industries in which the US firms are active. Further work in the UK[9] has suggested that US owned subsidiaries in the UK electronics industry have not been involved in the most highly advanced products, which have been developed in the US by the parent companies.

Selling prices. In determining prices, a recently established subsidiary of a foreign company is likely to stand outside any network of 'tacit understandings' or 'rules of the game', established among domestic firms, but this separation will diminish with time — a view presented in greater detail by Caves.[11] The price strategy of the new multinational will be based partly on experience in other countries, and its assessment of the probable sensitivity, ('elasticity'), of demand to price changes. Oligopoly theory would predict that a newly established foreign subsidiary would tend to fix prices fairly close to those of existing firms, unless there were a belief that existing firms would be unable to match an aggressive low price policy, or that the products of the new multinational entrant were sufficiently distinct to bear high prices, which could be supported by the firm's marketing skills.

Prices of numerous products differ substantially between countries within the EEC. Surveys of retail prices by the Commission of the European Communities were summarised in 1978,[12] and the summary revealed some remarkable variations in the prices of the same branded products. Much of this evidence on price divergences is incomplete — survey dates do not coincide and there is insufficient information in local competitive conditions. One thorough survey reported by the Commission in 1980[13] examined the retail prices of a large, (identical), sample of classical gramophone records in member countries, in November 1978, and found that retail prices, (including and excluding indirect tax), varied in relation to those of the UK as follows:

	Excluding Tax		Including Tax
UK	100	(Index base)	100
Belgium	143		165
France	110		136
Germany	147		152
Italy	104		110
The Netherlands	134		146

The Commission Report states that these countries can be divided into 'monopoly' markets, (Belgium, Germany, the Netherlands), and 'competitive' markets, (the UK, France and Italy), but since the same companies are competing in all six countries, this reasoning is hard to follow. The same companies may compete through prices in one market while they avoid starting price wars elsewhere. Once price competition has begun, as it did in the supply of gramophone records in the UK in the 1960s, it is very difficult to end. In examining the results of the EEC survey one may ask why, since both markets are dominated by the same few companies, the UK record prices were not raised to the level of those in Germany. This example may suggest the vulnerability of the multinational oligopoly enterprise rather than its dominance.

The determination of price by a multinational company will be influenced by the nature of the product, as well as the number and closeness of substitutes. Vaupel[14] concluded from his investigation of US multinationals that many of their products were among those on which consumers and business purchasers spent discretionary income, (with a high 'income elasticity of demand'). This is consistent with the observation that most of them are new and developing products rather than staple items. The demand for such 'discretionary' or 'luxury' products may, in general, be expected to be quite sensitive to price changes. Examples are: prepared and frozen foods, soft drinks and many durable goods. This last group includes products of which prices have risen only slowly or even fallen in recent years. For example, the ownership of many domestic electrical appliances has now reached saturation levels in most European countries, and sales depend on: (a) replacements; or (b) purchases of improved products, of further, (marginally less useful), units or of products which are considered less essential. Decisions to replace an electric cooker which works efficiently but is old fashioned in style; to replace a semi-automatic washing machine with a fully automatic one; to acquire a second TV receiver; or to acquire a video tape-recorder for domestic use are all likely to be very sensitive to price.

In the electrical and electronics industry multinational companies have played a major role in the introduction of new products, more economic methods of manufacture and *lower prices* which have stimulated demand. Competition between the few major competitors has been a major stimulus to this innovation. In contrast, one can point to the pharmaceutical industry as a sector where insensitivity of demand to price appears to have been exploited by international companies. Product improvements have been associated with higher prices. Many drugs are selected by people other than those who ultimately pay for them, which is one reason for price insensitivity. In all decisions relating to medicines there is a tendency to opt for 'the best which can be afforded'.

To summarise on prices, a distinctive feature of the multinational company is its probable greater ability, (from experience elsewhere), to assess the price sensitivity of demand for a product; whether it can exploit this depends upon local conditions and also upon the strategies of its competitors. Many of the industries in which multinationals are strongly represented are oligopolistic in nature. Once price competition has begun in such industries it is difficult for companies to bring it to an end.

Transfer pricing. Multinationals have, unless otherwise prevented, the power to fix the level of prices applying to international trade between subsidiaries, and to deviate from the prices which would be applied to outside companies, i.e. arms length transaction prices. The main inducements for multinationals to transfer goods or services at prices different from an arms length transaction price are:

(a) To manipulate reported profits in each country in order to exploit different tax rates.

(b) To minimise the amount of customs duties payable, particularly for import duties.

(c) To enable profits or capital to be repatriated.

The principles governing transfer pricing, its effects on the multinationals themselves and the implications of 'distorted' prices on general economic welfare have been extensively covered in the literature – the work by Plasschaert[15] provides a comprehensive analysis of these issues.

The factual evidence on transfer pricing is less easily available. The subject is surrounded by commercial security, and evidence becomes available only through the published findings of an official investigation with legal powers to enforce disclosure. Since such investigations are often initiated because there is *a priori* evidence of abuse, a study confined to such evidence might overstate the degree to which multinationals exploit transfer pricing. Examples where the official investigation concluded that transfer pricing artificially reduced profits in the host country, (the UK), are the Monopolies Commission's investigations of the household detergent industries[16] in 1966, and of the supply of tranquillisers[17] in 1973. In the case of the detergent manufacturers Procter and Gamble, the Commission considered that remittances to the US parent for transfer of research and development were excessive. In the case of tranquillisers, Hoffman La Roche, (the Swiss parent), achieved a high profit from UK operations by charging a high transfer price to the UK subsidiary for raw materials. On the other hand, the National Board for Prices and Incomes, also in the UK, found that the profits of Esso Chemical Ltd., (a subsidiary of Exxon), were artificially increased by the low transfer price of certain materials. (This last case is quoted by Dunning.[18])

Planned obsolescence. An increase in the cost and an apparent decrease in the availability of repairs, (an activity from which some multinationals have withdrawn), has been connected with the saturation of the markets for certain durable goods. This is partly due to the greater relative cost of labour intensive repair activities compared with the manufacture of new equipment, a disparity which has increased with greater manufacturing productivity.

The deliberate limitation of life of some goods — by the withdrawal of supply of spare parts, absence of servicing or even initial structural weakness — has been revealed by investigations of the Monopolies Commission of the UK and similar bodies. How far are such practices more pronounced among multinational companies? This question is difficult to answer, because the complaints presented in the last paragraph relate to industries which are dominated by multinationals. Planned obsolescence and multinational business occur in the same activities, but it seems unlikely that multinationalism increases planned obsolescence or the tendency towards replacement rather than repair.

Foreign trade and multinational companies

The effects of multinational operation on the balance of payments of the host country are difficult to predict. The transfer of production into a country may mean a substitution of domestic output for imports, but the importance of this depends on the previous level of imports. The ratio of value added within the country to the imports of materials and components, per unit of output, is also important. The establishment of a car assembly plant within a small, less developed economy might even lead to a deterioration in that country's balance of payments if it sold only to an expanded domestic market, since final assembly accounts for only about 25% of the total value of a car. This is why such countries are also eager to attract producers of components and of basic materials, including steel.

The impact of multinational companies on foreign trade is particularly important to developing countries and almost all published research on this subject has focused on developing economies. Within the developed economies of Europe this subject attracts less attention.

In the UK, subsidiaries of foreign manufacturers export a higher proportion of sales than other manufacturing companies. We analysed data for the 285 manufacturers among the 500 largest companies in the UK in 1977 − 78, based on company accounts for 12 months ended at any time during 1976 − 77. The results, derived by multiple regression described in Appendix II, show that on average the foreign owned firm is likely to derive nearly 9% more of its turnover from exports than a UK owned firm with the same total sales. The regression equation also showed that the export share tended to fall as turnover increased. Analysis by industrial sector showed that a greater proportion of sales was exported by foreign firms than by UK owned firms, in ten out of the eleven sectors in which foreign firms participated. (The only exception was clothing and footwear, in which foreign participation was low.) In total, 17.5% of the total turnover of foreign owned firms was exported, 11.3% of that of domestic firms.

Evidence from France for 1976[19] showed that the total exports of foreign owned subsidiaries in manufacturing industry represented a lower proportion of their sales than the corresponding ratio for domestic companies. (Companies with no exports at all were excluded from the comparison.) More detailed analysis showed that the proportionate importance of exports increased with the size of the firm, in the case of French firms, but decreased in that of foreign firms.

Table 3.1

Exports as percentage of sales in French firms, 1976

No. of employees	Exports as % of sales revenue	
	Foreign owned	other
Less than 200	28.7	18.4
200 −	26.7	18.8
500 − 1999	21.7	23.3
2000 − and over	14.5	24.8
All companies	17.9	23.2

Source: STSI[18]

Analysis of the data by sectors of industry shows that in 18 of the 34 sectors, the export sales ratio was greater for French than for foreign owned, 'implanted', firms but in the other 16 the reverse was true. The commentary by François, Mathieu and Suberchicot, authors of the French report, attributes the negative correlation between size of foreign enterprise and exporting to the different natures of the small and large 'implanted' enterprise. The small firm tends to be part of a wider operation where production is segmented between countries with a high rate of exports and imports. The larger firm tends to be more integrated.

There is an apparent contrast between our findings for the UK and those of the more extensive French research, (no data on exports are available for many German companies so that no comparative study could be made). Explanation of this contrast would require research beyond the scope of this current work but one factor may be the greater significance of exporting by US firms in the UK. Total sales by US owned firms in the UK in the three years 1974–76 were $79 billions compared with those of US firms in France of $47 billions. US subsidiaries in the UK exported 27.3% of their sales over the three years; those in France exported 21.7%. The French research team went on to examine the role of foreign owned subsidiaries as importers.[19] Their analysis had to overcome severe data problems but they were able to conclude that in 1976 foreign owned subsidiaries had a higher rate of imports per franc of exports, than French companies.

If foreign owned subsidiaries export a lower proportion of their turnover and have a higher import/export ratio, one may be tempted to conclude that their presence worsens a country's balance of payments, especially since there are also net transfers to the home country for use of headquarters facilities and remittance of profits. This conclusion cannot be reached because if the foreign firms were not present in the country concerned, imports might be considerably greater.

Studies by Hufbauer and Adler,[20] carried out in the early 1960s indicated that, after ten years, US direct investment in Europe would have a negligible net effect on the balance of payments of the host country: remittances to the USA would offset a positive balance of trade effects. An exception is where the direct investment from the US replaced a possible investment from a local source, in which case the balance of trade effect could also be negative. American domination of the European computer industry may well be an example of the latter kind. The UK National Economic Development Office estimated that activities of foreign multinationals in the UK computer industry had a negative net effect on the balance of payments of £200 millions in 1978, a continuation of a previous deficit.

Integration with one enterprise. We have already referred several times to the growing practice among companies with factories in different countries of the EEC, of organising production on an all European basis. Such organisation can take two forms — local specialisation on individual product lines or stages of production, or parallel production in different countries from which output is pooled.

The practice of specialisation is most likely in those activities with substantial opportunities for economies of scale of production; it is also adopted where particular products or production processes are suited to individual locations for reasons of quality or cost. For example, labour intensive activities would be sited in areas where employment is subsidised or where labour is in plentiful supply. The establishment of car assembly plants in southern Italy, Spain and the Irish Republic illustrates this last factor. Parallel production is undertaken where transport costs of the finished product are high but it is not confined to such products. It provides an opportunity to adjust to changing demands for individual products and reduces dependence on supplies and production continuity within a single area. The best known example, already quoted, is the motor industry but similar parallel production also takes place in other industries, including chemicals, tyres and many engineering and electrical products.

International agreements between multinationals. In any industry which is dominated by a few large firms there is a mutual incentive for these to reach agreements to refrain from, or at least to confine competition. Such agreements, which may be tacit rather than explicit, are more likely to affect competition through price than through advertising or product innovation. They may, however, relate to the boundaries of the activities of the companies concerned — either geographically or in terms of product. It should be emphasised that, unless they lead to formal merging, such agreements are subject to constant strain, usually because one company gains more than the other.

One agreement to restrict competition was that between AEG-Telefunken and the Italian domestic appliance firm Zanussi. The two firms reached agreement at the end of 1970 and the German firm acquired 20% of the equity of Zanussi in 1973 (sold in 1977). The agreement restricted the freedom of Zanussi to widen its product range, in so far as this would have meant competition with AEG-Telefunken; the latter company agreed to restrict its own activities in areas then dominated by Zanussi. The acquisition by AEG of further shares in Zanussi, (giving it majority control), was prohibited in 1974 by the German Cartel Office, explicitly because this would have given it power to withhold supplies of many of the inexpensive Italian imports which were holding down prices in the German markets.

The existence of joint equity holdings by European multinationals, is a feature of some of the national industries examined in Chapter 2. In food processing, in some parts of domestic electrical appliances, and in paper product manufacture, numerous examples of joint subsidiaries were encountered; some of them were owned equally by the two firms, (50% of equity), others split so that one company had a majority holding. For example, Unilever and Nestle were represented in the German frozen food industry at the time of the survey for the Commission, via a joint subsidiary, which had resulted from a merger. In this German company, Unilever had a majority holding. Meanwhile in France, Unilever has not entered either the frozen food or ice cream markets on any significant scale, again avoiding competition with Nestle. Another example of a joint subsidiary of companies based in different countries, is the gramophone record firm Polygram, which is jointly owned by Philips of Holland and Siemens of Germany. In this same market a formal agreement between Decca and AEG-Telefunken provides a major competitor in Europe to Polygram and its subsidiaries. There are fewer examples of participation of US firms in joint ventures in Europe or in formal agreements with European multinationals relating to competition in Europe. Some exist, such as the Bowater-Scott Corporation in the UK paper industry. There are also some minority holdings by US enterprises in major competitors in Europe — for example the US firm General Electric Inc. has a 10% holding in AEG-Telefunken.

The trade recession affecting the European economy in 1980 — 81 has emphasised the difficulties of predicting behaviour in oligopolistic markets with excess capacity. Theories developed over the past 40 years would suggest that under such conditions interdependence and common adversity would discourage firms from competing in many respects, and encourage agreements to safeguard existing market shares and margins. Instead, there appears to have been intensive competition not only through advertising but also through product innovations and prices. It is too early to draw definitive and quantified conclusions from the events of recent months, but there are indications that this competition may have been intensified by its international character.

Implications for public policy

The power of multinational enterprises in relation to governments

Any additional bargaining strength, in relation to national institutions, enjoyed by a company because of its multinational operations, rather than its size, must be derived from its ability to move production between countries. The greater the degree of concentration, the greater is the

70

importance to the host country of the individual multinational firm. Withdrawal or reduction of operations by an established multinational company might mean significant loss of employment and, if local production were replaced by imports, a substantial deterioration in the balance of external payments.

As the size of its operations within a country increases, the multinational's commitment to that country also increases. It becomes less easy to withdraw from that commitment, since there would be greater difficulty in the disposal of fixed assets and, depending on the particular country, there might be considerable expense in redundancy payments to employees, if the local subsidiaries could not be sold as going concerns. The position of the Chrysler company in the UK in the mid 1970s provides an interesting case study of the potential costs of withdrawal. The power of multinationals *vis à vis* national governments is probably greatest when the companies are expanding and therefore have options on the geographical location of their expanded activities. Some examples of this power follow in the more detailed consideration of public policies.

Within Europe there have often been allegations that governments have competed to attract multinationals. Once the political decision has been taken to encourage expansion by foreign owned firms, there is generally a move to offer tax concessions, subsidies or other assistance. Although within the EEC, the type and scale of such assistance is limited by agreement between member countries, some of these countries offer greater financial incentives than others to foreign multinationals. The scale of assistance in Great Britain, Ireland and Belgium has in the past received criticism. The power of home based multinationals is more restricted because the ability to transfer abroad may be limited by foreign exchange controls, and the company depends more on the goodwill of government and organised labour than a foreign owned firm. The bargaining power derived from multinationality is therefore smaller for the home based firm than for the foreign owned subsidiary.

During the period of low economic growth and recession during the later 1970s and 1980– 81, there has been some disinvestment in Europe both by US firms and by firms based in other European countries. Certain authors have argued that multinational companies are more likely to disinvest from host countries than local firms, (e.g. [20]). The basis of this argument has been the comparative mobility of the multinational firm and the changing relative merits of different locations.

In the EEC a new reason for disinvestment now appears to have emerged — unemployment at home. At the time of writing, the major British owned vehicle manufacturer, BL, has proposed the closure of its plant in Belgium while PSA-Peugeot-Citroen is negotiating with the UK government about the closure of one or more Talbot plants in Great Britain. Within countries, it is branch factories that tend to be closed during periods of recession. If an international dimension is added, there is great pressure on companies to 'save jobs at home' by curtailing foreign, rather than domestic operations. The long awaited 'rationalisation' expected to result from European integration and the abandonment of tariff restrictions may, rather anomalously, be brought about by national political pressures of this kind.

Policy in relation to 'fair trading' and consumer protection

In the second section on 'Business and competitive strategies of multi-national firms', we discussed the behaviour of multinational firms in concentrated industries, in relation to advertising, product innovation, prices and planned obsolescence. In many cases, the policy on such matters which best suits the financial interests of the multinational firm, will also be to the advantage of consumers in the host country. Examples are the introduction of new products and new methods of production, often accompanied by a general lowering of prices to encourage demand.

There are some situations in which the financial interests of the firm and those of the consumers may conflict — for example in the fixing of prices in 'captive' market segments, in the scale of advertising expenditure in fairly static oligopolistic markets, and in the length of life of some durable goods. In the UK the Monopolies and Mergers Commission concluded that the pricing policies of the multinational companies were not in the public interest in a number of cases, including colour photographic films, household detergents and, (perhaps the best known case because it was so fiercely contested), tranquillisers. In the case of household detergents, the Commission recommended substantial cuts in the scale of advertising expenditure and the lowering of prices. The best known case relating to durable goods concerns the life of electric light bulbs, also produced by multinational companies throughout Europe with agreements on designed life.[22]

One of the theoretical advantages of common markets covering large geographical areas, is the elimination of monopoly positions in individual countries. Competition from outside a country means that market segments are no longer captive. The simultaneous occurrence of concentration and multinational business, to some extent diminishes this competition because the same companies tend to predominate in different national markets. An international oligopoly emerges in some sectors, which is difficult for national governments to control. The 1978 report of the Directorate General for Competition concluded: 'The inter-penetration and internationalisation of markets in the Community seem, on the one hand, to have weakened some national monopolistic positions and, on the other hand, to have increased the degree of oligopoly, by restricting the number of firms operating in these markets.'[12]

Industrial and social policies of governments

In all European countries, governments intervene in varying degrees in industrial affairs in order to achieve conformity with their economic and social objectives. These objectives vary not only between countries but also between political parties within countries. One problem facing foreign multinational companies in some countries is hostility towards them on the part of some political groups and enthusiastic support on the part of others. The threat of expropriation of assets without compensation is probably small in most European countries. The possibility of compulsory state takeover with financial compensation remains, but is unlikely to occur without substantial warning. More frequent problems for all companies are probably caused by changes in policies on matters such as prices and income controls, employment protection, restrictions on permitted hours of work, regional industrial distribution, as well as the more obvious example of taxation and company affairs.

To some degree, the multinational company is better able to adapt to changes in national industrial policies, because these do not affect the totality of its operations. It is occasionally possible for a foreign multinational, in particular, to pursue a strategy against the policy of a national government, unless the latter is prepared to introduce and enforce laws to support that policy.

A recent example in the UK illustrates very clearly both the bargaining power of a foreign multinational firm in its relations with a national government, and also the difficulties faced by a government in applying an industrial policy which conflicts with the interests of a multinational firm. The case concerned the Ford Motor Company in the autumn of 1978. Since 1975 the British Government had enforced control over wage increases by discriminating against companies which infringed its stipulated norms, in the placing of public purchases and in the granting of discretionary aid under legislation, such as that relating to local employment creation. This control had been fairly effective with only a few exceptions. During 1978 Ford announced that a new commercial vehicle factory would be built in South Wales, an area of high unemployment and some political sensitivity. Considerable discretionary assistance was to be given by the Government, which presumably had to compete with other European governments also concerned about unemployment. From August 1978 the Government announced that the 'guideline' for pay increases was to be 5%, and in October 1978, Ford offered this increase to its employees as the annual pay settlement. This was refused; there was eventually a strike and finally in November 1978 the unions agreed to an offer by Ford which provided an average increase of about 14%, including an element which would be forfeited if attendance was irregular, (unofficial industrial action etc.). What would the Government do? Instruct all public authorities not to buy Ford vehicles? This would be difficult because that might mean uneconomic mixing of fleets, (fleet standardisation reduces maintenance costs), and also an increase in imports. Would the Government withdraw promised assistance for a new Welsh factory? This would hurt South Wales and the Government's popularity much more than it would hurt Ford, who would have been welcomed elsewhere in Europe. The Government appears to have accepted its inability to take sanctions against Ford; the matter was debated in Parliament and a motion criticising the incomes policy based on sanctions was approved. The final effect was a series of strikes aimed at rises approximately equal to that of Ford. It was this economic disruption which, in the view of most observers, brought about the defeat of the Government in Parliament and subsequently in the general election of May 1979.

This last case study is an extreme example of the power of a multinational company; the circumstances were in many respects unusual — a government which was close to the end of its term of office; a policy bitterly resented by many trade unionists and by employers; the political sensitivity of South Wales, where the Labour Party had earlier lost ground to the Welsh Nationalists in local elections.

In contrast, the limitations to the political power of multinational companies are illustrated by the recent history of resistance by US owned subsidiaries to West German legislation, giving greater power to employees in the management of the company. In 1976, representation of employees on the supervisory boards of companies was increased by law to 50%, with a shareholder chairman holding a casting vote. The application of this law to them was strongly resisted by some US companies and the American Chamber of Commerce was instrumental in a challenge to the law in the Constitutional Court. This case was decided in the government's favour during 1979. A 1979 article[23] described how this law led to substantial boardroom problems within Adam Opel, the German subsidiary of General Motors. These related particularly to the priority to be given to such issues as the shorter working week. Worker directors demanded the resignation of the personnel director and claimed their right to participate in the appointment of his successor. Despite these problems, it seems likely that General Motors will remain within Germany because their German plants are among their most productive and profitable. In such circumstances, a multinational company will probably prefer to accept unpalatable legislation, rather than withdraw.

Notes

1   See: Business Statistics Office, *Census of Production 1977, Summary Tables*, HMSO, London, 1980.

2   See: STISI, *L'implantation étrangère dans l'Industrie au 1 er janvier 1978*, publication no. 18, Documentation Française, Paris, 1980.

3   See: Van den Bulcke, D., *Les entreprises étrangères dans l'industrie belge*, University of Ghent, 1971, *De buitenlandse ondernmingen in de Belgische industrie*, seminaire voor toegpaste economie, Rijkuniversitet Gent 1971.

4   See: Deutsche Bundesbank, *The level of direct investment at the end of 1976*, Monthly Report, Volume 31, No. 4, Frankfurt-am-Main, April 1979.

5   See: Fishwick, F. and Harling, C.J., *Shiftworking in the Motor Industry*, National Economic Development Office, London, 1974.

6   See: *Advertising Age Europe,* Crain Communications Inc., London, 25 June 1979, pp. 16–20.

7   Source: 'The Top 50 Advertisers' in *The 100 Largest Companies in Britain, 1977–8*, Edited by Margaret Allen, Times Newspapers Ltd., London, 1979.

8   See: Vernon, R., 'International investment and international trade in the product cycle', *Quarterly Journal of Economics*, Vol. 80, 1966, reprinted in Dunning, J.H. (ed.), *International Investment*, Penguin Books, Harmondsworth, 1972.

9   See: Hood, N., and Young, S., *The Economics of Multinational Enterprise*, Longman, Harlow, 1979.

10   See: Dunning, J.H., 'The determinants of international production', *Oxford Economic Papers,* Vol. 25, OUP, Oxford, 1973.

11   See: Caves, R.E. 'Industrial Organisation' in Dunning, J.H. (ed.), *Economic Analysis and the Multinational Enterprise*, Allen and Unwin, London, 1974, pp. 115–46.

12   See: Commission of the European Communities, *Seventh Report on Competition Policy*, Brussels, 1978.

13   See: Commission of the European Communities, *Ninth Report on Competition Policy,* Brussels, 1980.

14   See: Vaupel, J.W., *Characteristics and Motivations of the US Corporations which Manufacture Abroad*, Atlantic Institute, Paris, 1971, (quoted by J.H. Dunning in reference 6).

15   See: Plasschaert, S., *Transfer Pricing and Multinational Corporations*, Saxon House ECSIM, Farnborough, 1979.

16   See: Monopolies Commission, *The Supply of Household Detergents* HMSO, London, 1966.

17   See: Monopolies Commission, *The Supply of Chlordiazepoxide and Diazepam,* HMSO, London, 1973.

18   See: Dunning, J.H., 'Multinational Enterprises, Market Structure, Economic Power and Industrial Policy', *Journal of World Trade Law,* Twickenham, 1974.

19   See: François, J.E., Mathieu, E., and Suberchicot, M., 'Investissement Etranger en France et Exportation' in *Les Exportateurs de l'industrie,* publication no. 4, STISI, Paris, 1980.

20   See: Vernon, R., *Sovereignty at Bay,* Longman, Harlow, 1971, (See page 183 for this unpublished report by Hufbauer and Adler).

21   See: Van den Bulcke, D., 'The Motives for Disinvestment from EEC Countries', in ECSIM, *Investment and disinvestment policies of multinational corporations in Europe,* Brussels, 1979.

Liebhaberg, B, *'Relations industrielles et entreprises multinationales en Europe',* Presses Universitaires de France, Paris, 1980, p. 39.

22   See: Guenault, P.H. and Jackson, J.M., *The Control of Monopoly in the United Kingdom,* Longman, Harlow, 1974.

23   See: Economist Intelligence Unit, *Paradoxes of Motor Industry in Germany,* Multinational Business, 1979 – No. 3.

4 Conclusions and implications for the future

Summary of conclusions

One reason for interest in industrial concentration is that it gives some indications about the degree and nature of competiton in the markets supplied. We explained in Chapter 1 that these indications are far from exact — there are problems of definition of the market and of concentration itself. The links between concentration indices and the 'abuse of dominating position' referred to, but not defined in Article 86 of the Treaty of Rome, are very tenuous. Only empirical investigation in each industrial sector can provide a satisfactory view of competition in the production markets.

There are also economic implications in concentration of employment and the purchase of intermediate products. The importance of such concentration depends on the degree of specialisation involved — how dependent are people with particular skills, or in particular areas, or people supplying particular products for a small number of firms? The evidence presented in Chapter 2 showed that some industrial sectors, particularly older industries with economies of scale in production, are highly concentrated and have very few firms producing outside their country of origin. In those national markets where local production provides substantial advantages over importing, particularly if economies of scale in production are limited, a high degree of multinational participation may exist with a low degree of concentration. The tendency for multinational firms to follow each other into such industries has been noted.

The statistical analysis of the UK and French data in Chapter 2 showed fairly weak but statistically significant positive correlations between foreign penetration and concentration in the analysis both of product markets, ('branches' in the French terminology), and industrial sectors. The application of multivariate analysis to the UK data showed that foreign participation had no additional influence on concentration when it was included in a model incorporating plant size, the plants per enterprise ratio and the size of the industry. Further analysis of the French data also showed that much of the correlation between foreign penetration and concentration could be explained by the positive association of each with economies of scale. German data were available only for simple correlation between foreign participation and concentration. Although this correlation was again statistically significant, there may be similar indirect explanations of this. The analysis of data for the UK and France tended to refute the theory that multinational operations and concentration were causally related. In neither country was there any trace of correlation between changes over time in the two variables. In the UK there was indeed a negative relationship between the level of foreign participation in each industry and changes in product concentration − over the two periods 1963 − 68 and 1968 − 75. Again, this correlation does not appear to be causal: non-British firms are most strongly represented in expanding activities, and increases in concentration are generally associated with contraction.

In Chapter 3 we identified four distinctive features of foreign subsidiaries in multinational companies − they are less vertically integrated than national firms, they operate very few small plants, they generally have higher rates of productivity, and pay higher wages than domestic companies in the same industries. We then examined the distinctive behaviour of multinational firms with regard to competition in national markets. We found that advertising by multinationals was no greater in relation to sales than that by other firms selling the same products − heavy advertising is a characteristic of many of the industries in which multinational companies are most prominent. On pricing, one distinctive feature of the multinational company is the greater opportunity to vary price according to sensitivities of demand in different national markets. We pointed out that many of the products associated with multinationals are among those which consumers buy with discretionary income, and are likely to be price sensitive. We raised the question as to whether multinationality of producers might increase a tendency towards a shorter life for some durable goods.

Analysis of the effects of foreign participation on the national balance of payments of the host country, was inconclusive. The UK evidence showed that foreign owned companies exported more of their sales than domestic counterparts in the same industries; data for France showed an opposite conclusion. In particular, large subsidiaries of foreign multinationals in France export a significantly lower proportion of their output than French firms of an equivalent size. When one adds the observation that foreign owned firms in France also had a higher ratio of imports to exports, a significant negative influence on the balance of payments may be suspected. However, foreign owned subsidiaries may be producing import substitutes, and this may outweigh their negative impact. Almost all the research about multinationals and external payments has been concerned with less developed economies — the net effect of foreign direct investment on external payments of developed countries cannot be assessed without further empirical research.

In the final subsection of Chapter 3 on 'Industrial and social policies of governments,' we discussed the relations between multinational business and government. We described two contrasting cases — one where a multinational company appears to have thwarted the policy of a national government, another where resistance by foreign owned companies to such a policy has failed to prevent its implementation. In regard to competition policy, we suggested that control of abuse within an international oligopoly might require supra-national authorities, one of which is the Commission of the European Communities.

Possible future trends

The beginning of 1981 was a particularly difficult time from which to forecast the European economy. Most countries in the EEC were facing the worst recession since the Second World War. At the same time other developed capitalist countries were facing the dual problems of inflation and unemployment. Although some economists speak of 'cyclical upturn', the threat of further major shocks to the world economic system, like the oil price increases of 1974 and 1979, make the early 1980s a time of great uncertainty. Most forecasters in early 1981 expected that in the new decade there will not be prolonged economic expansion in Europe equal to that in the years up to 1973. This is more likely to be a period of adjustment to slower growth, both in domestic European markets and in the rest of the world — in both capitalist and socialist economies.

An assessment of previous concern about this subject

It is against this gloomy, (perhaps pessimistic), outlook that some of the fears expressed about the economic power of the multinationals will be considered. Such fears were widely expressed in the 1970s after a period of substantial US investment in the manufacturing industries of continental Europe, and of considerably increased industrial concentration in the UK. It is important to separate the two processes geographically. Comprehensive data on concentration were available only for the UK. Data on concentration for continental countries related mainly to establishments, (operating units), rather than enterprises.

Concentration in UK industry increased substantially during the ten years 1958 — 68, both in the aggregate and in most industrial sectors, (evidence for this was presented in Chapter 2), but this increase had little connection with foreign investment. Evidence presented in Chapter 2 and in the statistical appendix shows virtually zero correlation between changes in foreign participation, and in concentration. Indeed, concentration increased significantly less in the years 1963 — 68, in those industries in which foreign multinationals were already present. Increased concentration resulted largely from defensive mergers of domestic firms in industries such as steel, heavy engineering and textiles, which were adjusting to reduced demand and ·competition from imports.

The effects of foreign participation on concentration in the rest of Europe during the years before 1972 cannot be accurately assessed. Data did not exist. The positive correlation between foreign participation and enterprise concentration, revealed by data for France and Germany which has become available in very recent years, needs careful interpretation. The absence, (from analysis of French data), of correlation between foreign participation and *changes* in concentration in recent years is probably a more relevant observation.

It would be unwise for one, who himself is about to embark upon prediction, to quote the forecasts made ten years ago which now appear erroneous. The main theme of many such forecasts was that both concentration and multinational operation within Europe would increase until the economy was dominated by a relatively small number of multinational companies. These might then have greater power than governments to control the economy. In questioning these predictions I can point to evidence that:

1   Concentration is not increasing appreciably, at aggregate or sectoral level, in those countries for which data exist.

2   Multinational operation is no longer being extended within Europe — there may be evidence of withdrawal.

3   Competition in *oligopolistic* industries has occurred on a scale inconsistent with some of the theories which imply collusion in periods of common adversity.

Will concentration increase?

By 1968 the 100 largest companies accounted for 41% of net output in UK manufacturing, an increase from 32% in 1958. From 1970 to 1977 it changed very little. The simple, (unweighted), average of five firm employment concentration ratios in the 125 UK industries, for which comparisons can be made, remained virtually unchanged between 1968 and 1977* at around 48 or 49%. Over the ten years 1958 — 68 there had been an increase in this mean from about 38%. The process of concentration in UK manufacturing appears to have slowed down appreciably in recent years — a view which is supported by a decline in the number of horizontal mergers.[1]**

Data for France for the period 1972—76 did not indicate any major trend towards greater concentration. The unweighted mean four firm sales concentrated ratio of the 42 sectors, for which data were given, rose from 40 to 41% over the four year period. Most of this, (very slight), increase was due to the disappearance of very small companies.

The UK and French data suggest a stabilisation of industrial structure in each of the two countries. The hypothesis that this is true for most EEC countries is supported by evidence from the reports for the Commission of the European Communities, described in Chapter 2. Is this stabilisation of industrial concentration a mere hiatus in a process which will be resumed? Why has it occurred? The interruption of the previous upward trend in concentration in the UK industry, has attracted only limited comment, partly because it has only recently become apparent. Hart and Clarke[1] leave these questions unanswered. The commentary on the French data[2] draws attention to the recent slow growth of concentration, without asking why the change has occurred.

Perhaps in recent years there has been more questioning of the advantages of size to a company. A recent study[3] of the relationship between size and profitability of UK companies reached a similar conclusion to that of earlier studies — that any such relationship was weak but negative. While statistical problems in such studies are considerable, their results appear to refute the principle that size brings major advantages — the limit of economies of scale, (where the economist's average cost curve becomes horizontal), may well be exceeded in some cases. Political views on the desirability of large scale enterprise may also have changed. Some left-wing politicians fear the power of large corporations which are able to move operations internationally and thwart domestic policies, (see for example S.Holland[4];) among politicians of the right there have been shifts of opinion towards small enterprise.

In projecting current trends in concentration, one can only conclude

---

* The 1968 data were taken from Hart and Clarke.[1] Data for 1973 and 1977 were taken from the Census of Production for those years.

** See page 84 for notes.

that the increasing trend, evident in the UK and believed to exist else-where in Europe, appears to have ceased. There are no immediately obvious indications in the economic and political environment that it should be resumed in the near future.

Trends in multinational operation

Among projections based on events up to 1970 were that: by 1981 US companies would 'control 20 to 25 per cent of British manufacturing' and that '75 per cent of world manufacturing assets would be controlled by 300 companies'.* Data suggest that, as with concentration, there have been some changes in the trends apparent before 1970.

In the UK, the proportion of net output and employment attributable to foreign owned subsidiaries in general, and US subsidiaries in particular changed as shown in Table 4.1.

Table 4.1
Total foreign penetration in the UK

	% of total for manufacturing industries			
	Net output		Employment	
	US	Total	US	Total
1968	10.4	13.4	7.4	9.7
1973	11.4	14.6	8.2	10.8
1977	13.1	19.0	9.8	13.9

Sources: Census of Production for 1968, 1973 and 1977.

The data in Table 4.1 shows that between 1968 and 1977 the partici-pation of American owned firms in UK manufacturing, increased less rapidly than that by firms based in other countries. Over the nine years, the penetration of UK industry net output by firms with headquarters in foreign countries other than the USA, increased from 3.0 to 5.9%.

In France in January 1973, (1972 accounts), majority owned foreign subsidiaries accounted for 20% of sales and 14% of employment in French industry, (excluding food processing). By January 1978 these percentages had increased to 26 and 17% respectively.[5&6] In January 1973, the percentage of total employees within US owned subsidiaries was 6%; five years later the percentage had risen only to 7. As in the UK, foreign enterprises had grown in importance but the main source of this growth was enterprises based in other EEC countries, whose

* These predictions, ascribed to Dunning and Barber respectively, appear in S. Holland's book.[4]

share of employment in French industry rose from 4.3 to 6.8% over the five years.

The data for both France and the UK are consistent with a world wide trend noted in a 1980 article by Franko[7] who pointed to a decline in the share of major markets obtained by US firms. It could be argued that the growing importance of European multinationals within the EEC posed a serious threat to consumer welfare — that this reduced his choice even more than if the investment were from outside Europe. However, this argument would overlook the observation that concentration has not been increasing, and also, the absence of any correlation in cross sections of industries between the rates of growth of multinational participation and of concentration.

During the recession of 1980 — 81 there had been several instances of disinvestment or withdrawal by foreign companies from the countries of western Europe. Closure of US owned companies have occurred in all member countries of the EEC and there have also been closures of plants in other EEC countries by firms with headquarters within the Community. These cases are not yet reflected in summary statistics. The closure of plants in foreign countries is analogous to the closure of domestic 'branch factories' during a recession — it causes less disruption and is generally easier to achieve than the alternative of reducing operations at home. Since within the EEC there are now few *formal* barriers to trade, closure of plants in other European countries need not mean the complete loss of those markets, (though evidence presented in Chapter 2 suggests that some loss may result).

Competition may be greater with multinational operations

Most of the industries with multinational participation are dominated by a fairly small number of major companies — though this number can vary from one or two to around 20. We have shown that there is no correlation between changes in foreign penetration and concentration. Direct horizontal investment by multinationals does not appear to be associated with increased concentration — even over a number of years, (our analysis in Chapter 2 covered 12 years in the UK). The industries in which multinationals operate tend, by the nature of their products or production methods, to be oligopolistic The oligopoly does not result from multinational participation. Indeed, following the research results of Knickerbocker, quoted in Chapter 2, one might argue that multinational investment leads to fragmentation rather than concentration — that if multinationals did not invest in horizontal investments, national markets might be more *monopolistic*.

Economic theory predicts that under conditions of excess capacity, firms in oligopolistic markets will avoid competition — first in price but also in other forms of competition. They will recognise interdependence and will reach tacit agreements. Previous authors quoted in Chapter 2 have asserted that such agreements to refrain from competition may be less easy to reach and to maintain, when the parties concerned are five or more companies based in different countries. The economic interests of multinationals based in different countries are less likely to coincide than those of a smaller number of national firms.

During the recent recession Europe has witnessed a major upsurge in competition. Price cutting, increased advertising and product innovation have appeared in many oligopolistic markets with multinational involvement. Much statistical information about this period will not be available until after the end of 1982. I venture to suggest that analysis of this period will indicate that the presence of multinational companies, preventing effective restrictive agreements, has increased rather than restrained competition.

Notes

1   See: Hart P. and Clarke R.E., *Concentration in British Industry 1935–75*, National Institute Occasional Paper, National Institute of Economic and Social Research, London, 1980.

2   See: STISI, *La Concentration des Entreprises Industrelles de 1972 à 1976*, Paris 1979.

3   See: Whittington, G., 'The Profitability and Size of United Kingdom Companies, 1960–74', *Journal of Industrial Economics,* Vol. XXVII, No. 4, June 1980, B.H. Blackwell, Oxford.

4   See: Holland, S., *The Socialist Challenge*, Quartet Books, London, 1975.

5   See: *Economie et Statistique,* No. 72, Documentation Française, Paris, 1974, pp. 4–14.

6   See: STISI, *L'Implantation étrangère dans l'industrie au 1er janvier 1978*, Documentation Française, Paris, 1978.

7   See: Franko, L., 'What has become of the American Challenge?', *Challenge*, New York, March – April 1980, pp. 49–52.

Appendices

1 Measures of concentration used in this book

Measures of concentration are usually classified into two groups — absolute and relative. Simple examples demonstrate the distinction: the combined share of the total sales of an industry obtained by any four firms is an absolute measure; the combined share of 20% of the total number of firms is a relative measure. Relative measures reflect only the inequality of firms; they are not affected by the number of such firms in an industry. For example, a statement that 20% of firms obtained 80% of an industry's sales might refer to one firm out of five or to 100 firms out of 500. Several indices which have been developed for the measurement of concentration reflect both the inequality of size and the number of firms. In the analysis which follows, we are interested primarily in the role of multinational companies in concentrated industries and the most appropriate measures are those which reflect the strength of the largest individual firms. The three measures which are quoted in this report are:

The simple, absolute concentration ratio

In the studies for the Commission of the European Communities this is calculated for four, eight and ten firms. In the UK Government figures, the ratio is calculated for five firms; in France for four and eight; and in Germany for three, six and ten. (All of which complicates comparison.)

The Herfindahl-Hirschman index

This is the sum of the squares of the proportions of total sales, (or other variable), obtained by individual firms. This index is a more composite measure of concentration than the more widely used simple concentration ratio, because the information provided by the latter depends on the number of firms included. Because of the process of squaring market shares, the Herfindahl-Hirschman index is affected mainly by the size of the large firms within an industry and by the inequality between these large firms. The index has a maximum value of 1, (one firm controls an industry), and a minimum of $1/n$, where n is the number of firms, (all equal in size).

The hypothetical example in Table A1, illustrates the calculation of the Herfindahl-Hirschman index and the previous comments on its significance. In both cases the four firm concentration ratio is 70% and the eight firm ratio 90%. In industry A, the maximum possible value of the Herfindahl-Hirschman index is 0.1394, (the 10% of market obtained by the firms not listed, must be shared by at least ten firms); the maximum possible for industry B is 0.238. Although the Herfindahl-Hirschman index has been advocated by several authors, (see Chapter 1[18 & 19]), as particularly appropriate for the analysis of oligopoly, no single index can represent a unique distribution of company sizes. It is possible for two quite different industry structures to yield the same value of the index. Even if some comprehensive and unambiguous index could be designed, the analysis of concentration cannot be reduced entirely to numbers. Financial and managerial links between firms, agreements to restrict competition, and legal restraints on such agreements all affect the economic significance of concentration.

Table A1

Illustration of the Herfindahl-Hirschman index

Firms	Industry A		Industry B	
	% of total	(share)^2	% of total	(share)^2
1	20	0.0400	45	0.2025
2	18	0.0324	10	0.0100
3	17	0.0289	9	0.0081
4	15	0.0225	6	0.0036
5	10	0.0100	6	0.0036
6	6	0.0036	5	0.0025
7	3	0.0009	5	0.0025
8	1	0.0001	4	0.0016
	90	0.1384	90	0.2344

The Rosenbluth coefficient

The French data quoted in Chapter 2 include a Gini coefficient, which is a purely relative measure, varying from O when all enterprises are of equal size, to 1 when one enterprise accounts for an entire industry.

The Rosenbluth coefficient quoted in Chapter 2 for France, is an adjustment of the Gini coefficient to allow for the number of firms:

$$Q = \frac{1}{n(1-G)}, \text{ where n is the number of firms.}$$

High correlation is usually detected between the simple absolute concentration ratio and the Herfindahl-Hirschman index, with a less close correlation with the Rosenbluth coefficient. Since simplicity aids comprehension, we have used the absolute concentration ratio for most of this report — only where the use of H or Q produced more interesting results, have such results been quoted.

II Technical – statistical analysis

2 MULTINATIONAL COMPANIES AND THE PROCESS OF INDUS-TRIAL CONCENTRATION

Statistical analysis of the relationship between foreign participation and concentration

UK product data

Repeating the analysis by Steuer described in the text, we took data from summary table 44 of the 1968 Census of Production, showing for a large number of products the percentage of sales obtained by the five largest enterprises* and the percentage obtained by majority owned subsidiaries of foreign companies. 'Sales' comprise of goods produced in the UK and sold within the UK or abroad, (imports are not included). Data were available for 1963 and 1968.

Where comparative data were available, we also included product concentration ratios from the Business Statistics Office publication, *Statistics of Product Concentration of UK Manufacturers in 1963, 1968 and 1975*, (PQ 1006, 1979). No data are available on sales by foreign owned companies for any year later than 1968.

The following results are relevant to the conclusions stated in the

---

* An *enterprise* includes all subsidiaries in which the share of voting capital controlled exceeds 50%.

text:

C = Percentage of sales obtained by five largest enterprises
F = Percentage of sales obtained by foreign owned firms
S = Total sales of product (in £)
t values are in parenthesis throughout.

(a) Including products where F = 0:

$$C_{68} = 59.23 + 0.384 \; F_{68}$$
$$(33.7) \quad (5.37)$$
$$R^2 = 0.106 \quad 244 \text{ observations}$$

The coefficient of F_{68} is significantly greater than zero, at 0.1%.

(b) Excluding products where F = 0:

$$C_{68} = 56.59 + 0.450 \; F_{68}$$
$$(24.2) \quad (5.70)$$
$$R^2 = 0.163 \quad 169 \text{ observations}$$

The coefficient of F_{68} exceeds 0 at the 0.1% significance level.

Changes in concentration 1963–68 (208 observations throughout). In this part of the analysis, the exclusion of product groups with F = 0, slightly reduced the significance of all independent variables, simply by reducing the number of degrees of freedom. (No results were affected.) The equations set out here therefore include *all* product groups for which data are available:

$$C_{68} - C_{63} \text{ versus } F_{68} - F_{63} \quad R^2 = 0.001$$

$$C_{68} - C_{63} = 5.05 - 0.040 \, (F_{68} + F_{63})$$
$$(7.38) \quad (2.76)$$
$$R^2 = 0.036$$

The coefficient of $(F_{68} + F_{63})$ exceeds 0 at the 1% level.

$$C_{68} - C_{63} = 9.34 - 0.040 \, (F_{68} + F_{63}) - 3.00 \; \frac{S_{68}}{S_{63}}$$
$$(5.81)(2.81) \qquad\qquad (2.94)$$
$$R^2 = 0.075$$

The coefficients of both independent variables exceed 0 at the 1% significance level.

$$C_{68} - C_{63} = 13.72 - 2.39 \, (S_{68}/S_{63}) - 0.105 \, C_{63}$$
$$(7.29) \quad (2.41) \qquad\qquad (4.87)$$

$$R^2 = 0.139$$

The coefficient of $\dfrac{S_{68}}{S_{63}}$ exceeds 0 at the 2% significance level, that of C_{63} at the 0.1% level.

$$C_{68} - C_{63} = 13.63 - 2.45 \, (S_{68}/S_{63}) - 0.095 \, C_{63} - 0.014 \, (F_{68} + F_{73})$$

$$R^2 = 0.142$$

The coefficient of $(F_{68} + F_{63})$ is not significantly different from zero.

Changes in concentration 1968 — 75 (157 observations)

$$C_{75} - C_{68} \text{ versus } F_{68} \quad R^2 = 0.019 \text{ (not significant)}$$

$$C_{75} - C_{68} = 7.84 - 2.21 \; \frac{S_{75}}{S_{68}} - 0.059 \; F_{68}$$
$$(5.52)(4.11) \qquad (2.23)$$

$$R^2 = 0.098$$

The coefficient of $\dfrac{S_{75}}{S_{68}}$ exceeds zero at the 0.1% significance level, that of F_{68} at the 5% level.

$$C_{75} - C_{68} = 13.03 - 1.88 \; \frac{S_{75}}{S_{68}} - 0.106 \; C_{68}$$
$$(7.26) \quad (3.60) \qquad (4.85)$$

$$R^2 = 0.167$$

The coefficients of both independent variables are significant at the 0.1% significance level.

$$C_{75} - C_{68} = 12.93 - 1.86 \; \frac{S_{75}}{S_{68}} - 0.100 \; C_{68} - 0.023 \; F_{68}$$
$$(7.18) \quad (3.55) \qquad (4.34) \qquad (0.85)$$

$$R^2 = 0.170$$

The coefficient of the additional independent variable (F_{68}) is not significantly different from zero.

Chi-squared test of significance of results in Table 2.11 Table 2.10 may be reproduced as follows:

Table A2.1

| Foreign share | Five firm concentration ratio | | |
%	Below 65%	Above 65%	Total
Zero	39	36	75
1 – 30	70	55	125
Above 30	9	55	44
Total	118	126	244

If the 75, 125 and 44 product groups in the three degrees of foreign participation were random samples of the total of 244 groups, then the expected proportion in the less than 65% concentration class would be $\frac{118}{244}$ in each case. These expected frequencies are shown in the parenthesis;

Chi-squared is then calculated as:

$$X^2 = \sum \frac{(f_o - f_x)^2}{f_x} \quad \text{where } f_o = \text{observed frequency}$$
$$f_x = \text{expected frequency}$$

Table A2.2

| Foreign share | Concentration ratio | |
(%)	Below 65%	Above 65%
Zero	39 (36)	36 (39)
1 – 30	70 (61)	55 (64)
Above 30	9 (21)	35 (23)

The value of Chi-squared is 16.19, which with two degrees of freedom is significantly different from zero at the 0.1% level. (The probability that the different distributions are due to chance is less than one in a thousand.)

UK industry data

Hart and Clarke specified and tested a model explaining concentration in each of 141 Minimum List Headings, (three digit industry classification), in the 1968 Census using the following form:

C = Estimated five firm concentration ratio for employment.

M = Florence Median plant size, ('The hypothetical plant at the mid-point of the array so that half of the employment of an industry comes from plants larger than this and half from smaller plants' — Hart and Clarke,[1] page 84).

P = Ratio of plants, (establishments), to enterprises.

Z = Total employment in the Minimum List Heading.

The estimation of the Florence Median was difficult in open-ended classes, that is where over half the employees in an industry were employed in establishments with a stated number of six and over. In such cases, we calculated a hypothetical distribution of establishment sizes by assuming that each establishment in the open class was, $(1 + k)$ times the next largest. The value of k was estimated by iteration, until:

$$\sum_{i=0}^{n} (\text{Lower boundary of class})(1 + k)^{i + \frac{1}{2}} = \text{Total employment (known)}$$

where n = number of establishments in class.

The same geometric principle was used for interpolation in other classes. Hart and Clarke used linear interpolation and in some cases extrapolation, which may be less accurate.

Our rather elaborate means of estimating the Florence Median (M) is probably the main reason why our retesting of Hart and Clarke's specification gave slightly better results than these authors' own test. Specification:

$$\text{Log } C = b_0 + b_1 \text{Log } M + b_2 \text{Log } P + b_3 \text{Log } Z$$

Table A2.3
Values of coefficients (all logs. to base e)

	Hart and Clarke (as quoted)		Fishwick (this study)	
	Coefficient	t	Coefficient	t
b_0	2.09	(16.0)	1.77	(14.3)
b_1	0.38	(19.0)	0.44	(21.0)
b_2	0.56	(05.6)	0.67	(06.6)
b_3	- 0.24	(12.0)	- 0.26	(12.0)
	$\bar{R}^2 = 0.783$		$\bar{R}^2 = 0.833$	

Having reproduced the data and analysis of Hart and Clarke, we proceeded to find out whether foreign participation in an industry had any independent effect on concentration. For this purpose, we calculated a new variable F — the sum of foreign companies' sales of principal products divided by the total sales of those products. In 31 of the 141 industries the coverage of products in the data on foreign participation was insufficient, and these were excluded from the analysis.

Two samples were then used to test whether F significantly affected C when included in a regression equation with M, P and Z as other independent variables. The first of these excluded industries where F = 0, (since a zero value prevented the use of Hart and Clarke's logarithmic transformation); the second included such values.

Results: (t values in parenthesis; all logarithms to base e)

1 Industries with zero values of F excluded
(No. in sample = 85)

$$\text{Log C} = 2.039 + 0.388 \text{ Log M} + 0.697 \text{ Log P} - 0.238 \text{ Log Z}$$
$$\qquad\quad (12.3) \quad (14.7) \qquad\quad (4.9) \qquad\qquad (9.5)$$

$$\bar{R}^2 = 0.806$$

$$\text{Log C} = 2.038 + 0.396 \text{ Log M} + 0.680 \text{ Log P} - 0.242 \text{ Log Z} - 0.011 \text{ Log F}$$
$$\qquad\quad (12.2) \quad (13.0) \qquad\quad (4.6) \qquad\quad (9.2) \qquad\qquad (0.5)$$

$$\bar{R}^2 = 0.804$$ (The introduction of log F as an additional variable has no significant effect)

2 Industries with zero values of F included
(No. in sample = 110)

$$\text{Log C} = 1.883 + 0.419 \text{ Log M} + 0.691 \text{ Log P} - 0.249 \text{ Log Z}$$
$$\qquad\quad (12.8) \quad (17.5) \qquad\quad (6.2) \qquad\qquad (10.5)$$

$$\bar{R}^2 = 0.814$$

$$\text{Log C} = 1.846 + 0.433 \text{ Log M} + 0.659 \text{ Log P} - 0.253 \text{ Log Z} - 0.0015 \text{ F}$$
$$\qquad\quad (12.2) \quad (15.9) \qquad\quad (5.7) \qquad\quad (10.6) \qquad\qquad (1.06)$$

$$\bar{R}^2 = 0.814$$ (The coefficient of F is again insignificant)

3 Further analysis of F in relation to other variables

The simple correlation coefficients between C and F were 0.225 when industries with zero values of F were included and 0.359 when these were excluded. This positive simple relation can be consistent with the absence of any partial relationship in the equations tested above only if F is related to the other independent variables.

Numerous linear and non-linear relationships between variables were tested. The following emerged as the equation giving the best explanation of F, using only 85 industries with non-zero values of F:

$$\text{Log F} = 0.664 \text{ Log M} - 1.567 \text{ Log P} - 0.328 \text{ Log Z} - 0.082$$
$$(5.14)(2.26)(2.67)(0.10)$$

$$R^2 = 0.268 \quad (\bar{R}^2 = 0.250)$$

(The inclusion of Log C as an additional variable had a negligible effect and its coefficient was not significant.)

Since F is significantly influenced by all three variables which together are closely correlated with C, a simple correlation between C and F is consistent with the conclusions of 1 and 2 in the previous results.

French data

Data for France were drawn mainly from reports published by the Service du Traitement de l'Information et des Statistiques Industrielles, (STISI), within the Ministère de l'Industrie. The principal publications used in this analysis are as follows:

1 STISI, '*L'Implantation Etrangère dans l'Industrie au 1er janvier ...*', (1975 then annually), in a series entitled '*Recueils Statistiques*', (Publication numbers 3, 9, 14 and 18). The latest data, published in October 1980, were for January 1978.

2 STISI, '*La Concentration des Entreprises Industrielles de 1979 à 1976*', also in '*Recueils Statistiques*', number 13. One problem with these data is a change in the system of industrial classification between the two dates. This prevents the comparison of concentration over a time, in detailed subsectors.

3 INSEE, *Les entreprises françaises: concentration et grandes entreprises des secteurs et des branches*, publication E64 of INSEE, June 1979. This contains considerable detail about concentration by industrial sector, and by product group, ('branche').

4 INSEE, *La Concentration des Etablissements Industriels en 1962 et 1972*, 1978. This is useful in providing direct data on plant sizes by industrial sector.

Product concentration. Product concentration data for 1975 were similar in definition to that for the UK, that is they refer to sales by producers in France, to home or export markets. There are no corresponding figures for foreign participation, but there is a list of the four largest firms in each of the 282 manufactured product groups for which the 1975 four firm concentration ratio is given. By checking the ownership of these firms we have been able to generate some data for comparison with concentration.

The first question investigated was whether there was any significant difference between concentration levels in product groups with no foreign owned company in the first four, and those in other groups. There was a foreign owned, (50%+), firm among the first four in 101 of the 282 groups. The following results were obtained:

C_4: Where first four French owned, (181 groups)   50.14
Where at least one of four foreign, (101 groups)   44.17

The standard deviation of C_4 in each of the two clusters was close to the overall standard deviation of 29.0. With such a high standard deviation, the difference between the means of the two categories is not significant — with a ratio of difference to standard error of 1.66.

We then decided to construct a variable from the information in the ranking of firms. For any product groups this new variable, which we shall call X, was the total of points accorded as follows:

4 points if the first enterprise in order of sales was foreign owned
3 points if the second enterprise in order of sales was foreign owned
2 points if the third enterprise in order of sales was foreign owned
1 point if the fourth enterprise in order of sales was foreign owned

Where between 20 and 50% of a company was owned by a single foreign enterprise we included in the new variable X, half the above weight, (e.g. if the second largest company was 25% owned by a foreign firm, 1½ points were added to the index). The index, (X), was then compared in two ways with the four firm concentration ratio:

1 Regression between product concentration and presence of foreign firms in first four

C_4 = Four firm concentration ratio

X is defined in immediately preceding paragraphs

$$C_4 = 44.4 + 1.61X \quad R^2 = 0.019$$
$$(2.31) \quad \text{282 observations}$$

The coefficient of X is significantly different from zero at the 5% level but the correlation is clearly very weak.

Only after considerable iteration was it possible to identify a classification which produced significant results, as shown in Table A2.4.

Table A2.4

C_4	Value of X (See previous paragraph)				
	Less than 4		4 and over		
Less than 30	90	+	13	=	103
30 - 49.9	53	+	16	=	69
50 - 79.9	51	+	11	=	62
80 and over	32	+	16	=	68
Total	226	+	56	=	282

The value of Chi-squared, against the null hypothesis that the samples of 226 and 56 product groups were random samples from the population of 282, was 9.52 which, with three degrees of freedom, is significant at 5%. As with the UK data, the main difference between the two clusters is the comparatively small number of activities with high foreign involvement and low concentration. Whereas nearly 40% of the 226 activities with little foreign participation had four firm sales concentration of under 30%, only 13 of the 56 other activities fell into this low concentration category. This difference was much less pronounced than in the UK.

Industry concentration—French industry, (Sectoral), data. The study of foreign participation by the STISI, excludes certain food processing industries; public utilities were included in the original survey but, because they have no foreign participation, do not appear in the final analysis. The STISI analysts define an 'index of foreign penetration', (Indice de Pénétration Etrangère or IPE) as follows:

If p represents the proportion of equity capital controlled by the foreign enterprise then the value of sales, employment or other variable V for any single firm i, to be included in the numerator of IPE, (see as follows), is S_i:

$S_i = V_i$ where $p_i > 0.50$ (that is the total value of the variable for firm i)

$S_i = p_iV_i$ where $0.50 \geq p_i \geq 0.20$ (the actual proportion of equity capital times the variable)

$$S_i = 0 \quad \text{where } p_i < 0.20$$

(since participation of less than 20% does not give any control)

$$IPE = \frac{\sum S_i}{\sum V_i}\ 100$$

Level comparisons in 1976

We calculated simple regression of 1976 concentration measurements on foreign participation, (IPE), using the mean of the published values for January 1976 and January 1977, for IPE.

Several indices of concentration were available from the French data, among them were: the four firm concentration ratio, (C_4); the Herfindahl-Hirschman index, (H); and the Gini coefficient, (G). We replaced the last of these measures, which reflects only the inequality of the size distribution by the Rosenbluth index, (Z), which, as explained in Appendix I, also takes into account the number of companies. The correlation coefficients between the various indices were themselves high, as shown in Table A2.5.

Table A2.5

Matrices of Correlation Coefficients between Concentration Measures
(Data for 34 French Sectors 1976)

	Employment C_4	H	R
C_4	1.000		
H	0.987	1.000	
Q	0.797	0.787	1.000

	Sales C_4	H	R
C_4	1.000		
H	0.980	1.000	
Q	0.761	0.816	1.000

The simple correlation between IPE and concentration was found to be highly significant whichever concentration index was used. (In all the equations — t values are in parenthesis, there were 34 observations and logarithms were to base e.)

Employment

$$C_4 = 14.36 + 0.722 \text{ (IPE)} \qquad R^2 = 0.227 \qquad \text{(a)}$$
$$\quad (2.54) \quad (3.06)$$

$$\text{Log } H = 1.16 + 0.552 \text{ (Log IPE)} \qquad R^2 = 0.269 \qquad \text{(b)}$$
$$\quad (0.46) \quad (3.43)$$

$$\text{Log } Q = 0.053 \text{ (IPE)} - 5.98 \qquad R^2 = 0.283 \qquad \text{(c)}$$
$$\quad (3.55) \qquad (15.45)$$

Sales (net of tax)

$$C_4 = 15.61 + 0.682 \text{ (IPE)} \qquad R^2 = 0.265 \qquad \text{(d)}$$
$$\quad (2.79) \quad (3.40)$$

$$\text{Log } H = 1.19 + 0.546 \text{ (Log IPE)} \qquad R^2 = 0.293 \qquad \text{(e)}$$
$$\quad (2.67) \quad (3.64)$$

$$\text{Log } Q = 0.050 \text{ (IPE)} - 5.83 \qquad R^2 = 0.304 \qquad \text{(f)}$$
$$\quad (3.74) \qquad (15.62)$$

With 32 degrees of freedom, all of the coefficients of the independent variable in equations (a) to (f) are significantly different from zero at the 1% level. Relationships (b), (c), (e) and (f) are represented diagrammatically in Figures A2.1 to A2.4 at the end of this Appendix. It can be seen that there are few industries with high values of IPE, and low concentration ratios.

Level comparisons in 1972

Some less detailed information on foreign penetration in 1972[1] showed little variation from the data published for 1 January 1975, (most of which referred to the calender year 1974). We decided to use the January 1975 estimates of IPE, together with data for 1972 on establishment sizes[2] to try to explain a higher proportion of concentration in 1972, than that achieved for 1976 in the previous equations (a) to (f) above.

Information on establishments related to employment, and the dependent variable chosen for analysis, was the four firm enterprise concentration ratio for employment.

1 see: Economie et statistique no. 72, Documentation Francaise, Paris 1974, (pp. 4–14).

2 See: INSEE, La Concentration des Establissements Industriels en 1962 et 1972, 1978, Paris.
This is described earlier in the Appendix.

Q_{1000} = proportion of employees in establishments with 100 + employees

Q_{500} = proportion of employees in establishments with 500 + employees

$$C_4 = 4.23 + 0.652\ Q_{1000} + 0.420\ IPE \qquad R^2 = 0.71 \qquad (g)$$
$$\quad\ (6.78) \qquad\qquad (2.54) \qquad (\bar{R}^2 = 0.68)$$

$$C_4 = 0.703\ Q_{500} + 0.311\ IPE - 6.36 \qquad R^2 = 0.81 \qquad (h)$$
$$\ \ (9.06) \qquad\quad (2.23) \quad\ \ (1.76) \qquad (\bar{R}^2 = 0.80)$$
$$n = 34$$

The correlation coefficient between Q_{1000} and IPE was 0.34, (just below 5% significance level), that between Q_{500} and IPE was 0.39, (above the 5% significance level).

There is opportunity for further analysis of the large volume of data published in recent years in France, which lies beyond the scope of this current project. We can conclude that foreign participation has an effect on concentration over and above the effect of economies of scale, (which themselves seem to have a limited effect), but that this effect is rather weak.

Changes in concentration 1972 – 76

French sectoral data permit a comparison of changes in concentration, (the four firm concentration ratios for sales and employment), with the values of IPE for employment in January 1975:

Employment: $\quad C_4 = 0.91 + 0.0066\ IPE_{emp.} \qquad R^2 = 0.001$
$$\qquad\qquad\quad (0.95)\quad (0.17)$$

Sales: $\qquad\quad C_4 = 0.53 + 0.0226\ IPE_{sales} \qquad R^2 = 0.010$
$$\qquad\qquad\quad (0.50)\quad (0.57)$$

Data for Germany

Concentration ratios for German industry were published for the first time in the 1977 statistics, in *Beschaftigung, Umsatz und Investitionen der Unternehmen im Bergbau und in VerarbeitendenGewerbe*. (Reihe 4, 2, 1 in official series published by the Statistisches Bundesamt in Wiesbaden). Values are given for C_3, C_6 and C_{10} for both employees, (beschaftigten), and sales turnover, (umsatz).*

---

* It should be noted that the 'enterprise', as defined in the German Statistical office data, does not include subsidiaries with separate legal identity. This means that German concentration ratios understate concentration compared with those for France and the UK, where financial control, (rather than legal identity), is the criterion for definition.

101

In April 1979 the Deutsche Bundesbank published the first comprehensive data on foreign investment in Germany — for 1976. Similar data for 1977 were published in April 1980. The Bundesbank has made available to us more detailed data showing foreign participation in each of the 29 sectors of manufacturing industry; concentration ratios were available for 27 of these sectors.

The Bundesbank analysts have estimated the shares of turnover and employment in each industry, obtained by enterprises with 'primary and secondary participations' by foreigners. 'Primary participation' occurs where 25% or more of the shares or voting rights of a German firm are owned by a foreign enterprise in the same activity. 'Secondary participation' occurs where this proportion of shares is held by a foreign based financial holding company. Unlike the French IPE (previously described), the German estimates of shares of variables do not distinguish between majority controlled subsidiaries, and those where the largest foreign shareholder owns between 20 and 50% of voting rights.

Linear equations produced the closest correlations between concentration and foreign participation in simple regression:

C represents the *six firm* percentage concentration ratio

F the proportion of the variable concerned attributable to foreign owned firms

t values are in parenthesis

For sales turnover $C = 14.1 + 82.5F$ $\quad R^2 = 0.56$
$$(5.60)$$

For employment $C = 12.7 + 90.4F$ $\quad R^2 = 0.52$
$$(5.13)$$

When multiple regression was used to explain inter-industry variations in concentration and foreign participation, logarithmic transformations, as suggested by Hart and Clarke, (see [38], page 54), were found to give the best results:

C = 6 firm concentration ratio (percentage)
F = share of foreign owned firms (proportion)
P = plants per enterprise in industry (arithmetic mean)
S = employees per plant (arithmetic mean)
Z = total employment in industry

t values in parenthesis

Sales turnover

$$\text{Log } C = 5.675 + 1.030 \text{ Log } P + 0.587 \text{ Log } S - 0.328 \text{ Log } Z \quad \text{(a)}$$
$$(1.29) \qquad\qquad (3.98) \qquad\qquad (3.05)$$

$$S^2 = 0.268 \qquad R^2 = 0.656$$
$$\bar{R}^2 = 0.611$$

$$\text{Log } C = 5.929 + 0.529 \text{ Log } P + 0.668 \text{ Log } S - 0.331 \text{ Log } Z + 0.126 \text{ Log } F$$
$$\qquad\qquad (3.33) \qquad\quad (0.76) \qquad\quad (3.08) \qquad\quad (0.97) \quad \text{(b)}$$

$$S^2 = 0.269 \qquad R^2 = 0.670$$
$$\bar{R}^2 = 0.610$$

[The inclusion of log F led to a very slight increase in S^2 and reduction in $\bar{R}^2$ compared with equation (a).]

$$F = 0.317 + 0.884 \text{ Log } P + 0.050 \text{ Log } S - 0.045Z \qquad\qquad \text{(c)}$$
$$\qquad (4.23) \qquad\qquad (1.28) \qquad\quad (1.61)$$

$$R^2 = 0.656$$
$$\bar{R}^2 = 0.611$$

Notes: 1 The use of F gave better results than that of Log F in equation (c)

2 Multicollinearity between the independent variables means that little valid interpretation of *partial* regression coefficients is possible.

Employment

$$\text{Log } C = 5.757 + 0.926 \text{ Log } P + 0.660 \text{ Log } S - 0.337 \text{ Log } Z$$
$$\qquad\qquad (1.14) \qquad\quad (4.41) \qquad\quad (3.10)$$

$$S^2 = 0.276 \qquad R^2 = 0.678$$
$$\bar{R}^2 = 0.636$$

$$\text{Log } C = 6.025 + 0.565 \text{ Log } P + 0.598 \text{ Log } S - 0.340 \text{ Log } Z + 0.129 \text{ Log } F$$
$$\qquad\qquad (0.63) \qquad\quad (3.62) \qquad\quad (3.11) \qquad\quad (0.91)$$

$$S^2 = 0.278 \qquad R^2 = 0.689$$
$$\bar{R}^2 = 0.632$$

(inclusion of Log F worsens, rather than improves, the result)

$$F = 0.277 + 0.690 \text{ Log } P + 0.054 \text{ Log } S - 0.033 \text{ Log } Z$$
$$\qquad (4.32) \qquad\qquad (1.82) \qquad\quad (1.54)$$

$$R^2 = 0.690$$
$$\bar{R}^2 = 0.633$$

(As with sales turnover, multicollinearity affects the *partial* regression coefficients)

3 CHARACTERISTICS AND BEHAVIOUR OF MULTINATIONAL FIRMS IN CONCENTRATED INDUSTRIES

The distinctive features of multinational firms

General methodology of statistical tests

The example of value added in relation to sales will be used to illustrate the general method applied in the first section of Chapter 3.

If Vf = Total value added by all foreign firms in a sector
Vd = Total value added by all domestic firms in a sector
Sf = Total sales of all foreign firms in the sector
Sd = Total sales of all domestic firms in the sector

It can be shown by manipulation that if

$$\frac{Vf}{Sf} = \frac{Vd}{Sd} \quad \text{then} \quad \frac{Vf}{Vf + Vd} = \frac{Sf}{Sf + Sd}$$

$$\text{Let } p = \frac{Vf}{Vf + Vd} \bigg/ \frac{Sf}{Sf + Sd}$$

If the sample of n sectors were random subsets of data, from a sample with equal average ratios of value added to sales among foreign and domestic firms, then the mean value of $p(\bar{p})$ would tend to 1 as n tended to infinity.

Tests of significance for $\bar{p} = 1$ were based on

$$t = \frac{(1 - \bar{p})(\sqrt{n})}{s}, \quad \text{where} \quad s = \sqrt{\frac{\Sigma (p - \bar{p})^2}{n - 1}}$$

It may be argued that if in one sector $p = 2$ and in another 0.5, the average of two ratios should be 1, (the geometric mean), rather than 1.25, (the arithmetic mean). This argument can be disputed: in order to avoid the choice, both p and log p have been checked in each significance test. (The use of log p instead of p in the computation of t, is equivalent to checking whether the geometric mean is significantly different from 1.)

In all the tests, the UK data referred to shares of each variable attributed to majority owned firms and other firms; the French data refer to the IPE, (index of foreign penetration), defined previously and applying to each variable.

Results

Table A2.6
Test

| | | t values | | | |
| | | UK (n = 15) | | France (n = 36) | |
Numerator		p	log p	p	log p
value added (V)	sales (S)	-2.34	-2.49	-6.00	-6.38
value added	employment	3.44	4.15	2.34	2.10
remuneration (operatives)	operatives	3.77	3.87	not available	
remuneration (other)	other employees	4.45	4.57	not available	
remuneration	all employees	(not calculated)		4.02	3.94

Note

Table A2.7
Significant levels of t

	14 degrees of freedom (UK)	35 d.f. (France)
5%	2.14	2.03
2%	2.62	2.44
1%	2.98	2.73
0.1%	4.14	3.60

Business and competitive strategies of multinational firms

The competitive strategies of multinationals

Advertising — company sales (UK data)

s = company's percentage share of total sales over period 1974—77 a = company's percentage share of advertising expenditure over same period

$$a = 0.92s - 0.52 \qquad R^2 = 0.81$$

$$\text{no. of companies} = 40$$

The sum of residuals for 16 foreign owned firms included in the total was not significantly different from zero — implying that their advertising pattern was similar to that of UK based firms. The equation suggests that a firm with 20% of sales would account for 17.9% of advertising; one with 40% of sales for 36.3%. (Data for the food and domestic appliances industries were pooled, because the totals of residuals for each group were close to zero.)

Foreign trade and multinational companies

For UK firms if:

T = turnover in £ billions (10^9)

X = export sales in £ billions

F = 1 if foreign owned firm, 0 if UK owned

$$\frac{X}{T} = \underset{(14.7)}{0.162} - \underset{(2.05)}{0.0199T} + \underset{(4.17)}{0.0859F}$$

$$R^2 = 0.074 \qquad n = 285 \qquad \text{t values in parenthesis}$$

The result implies that a foreign firm is likely to export 8.6% more of its turnover than a UK owned firm.

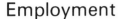

Employment

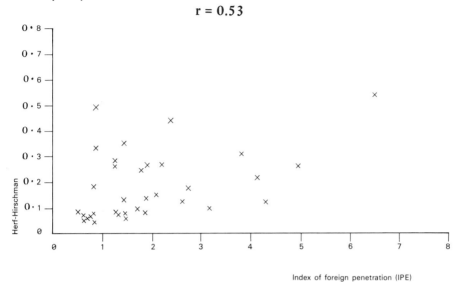

Figure A2.1 Concentration and foreign penetration
in France – Employment

Sales

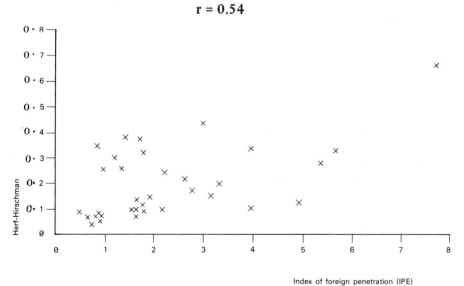

Figure A2.2 Concentration and foreign penetration
in France – Employment

107

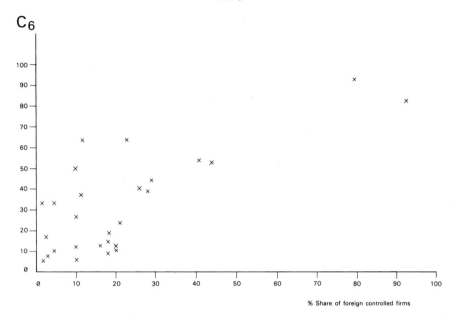

Figure A2.3 Sales concentration and foreign participation
in German manufacturing industries 1977

Note: 'Foreign-controlled firms' include those in which a single foreign
shareholder holds at least 25% of equity.

Sources: Statistiches Bundesamt
Deutsche Bundesbank

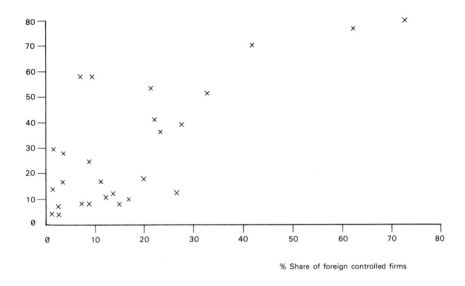

Figure A2.4 Employment concentration and foreign participation
in German manufacturing industries 1977

Note: 'Foreign-controlled firms' include those in which a single foreign
shareholder holds at least 25% of equity.

Sources: Statistiches Bundesamt
Deutsche Bundesbank

Index